REDEFINING OUR HOLINESS HERITAGE

RENEWING OUR MINDS, REFRESHING OUR LANGUAGE

You were taught, with regard to your former way of life,
to put off your old self,
which is being corrupted by its deceitful desires;
to be made new in the attitude of your minds;
and to put on the new self,
created to be like God in true righteousness and holiness.

The Apostle Paul
to us and to the church in Ephesus

REDEFINING OUR HOLINESS HERITAGE

RENEWING OUR MINDS, REFRESHING OUR LANGUAGE

Daniel E. LeRoy

Old Blue Truck Publishing Co.

Old Blue Truck Publishing Co.
708 Tar Heel Trail
Kernersville, North Carolina 27284

Old Blue Truck Publishing Co. is the self-publishing ministry of Daniel E. LeRoy.
pastordanleroy@gmail.com   (336) 813-5494

Special assistance provided by Timothy Kirkpatrick, **SECONDCHAIR** SOLUTIONS,
www.secondchair.solutions   (540) 212-9487

Cover Design: **SECONDCHAIR** SOLUTIONS

ISBN 9798872724186

Printed in the United States of America

DEDICATION

This book is dedicated to all the young Wesleyan preachers
who are hungry for holiness and still idealistic enough in your spirits
that you believe we can bring holiness back to the heart of
The Wesleyan Church.

I hope this book will fan the flame on the altar of your heart
and give you tools to better share the story in a compelling,
Spirit-anointed way with your generation.

CONTENTS

12

DISCLAIMER

The "Our Holiness Heritage" series
is published as a service to The Wesleyan Church
and a challenge for The Wesleyan Church.
The views expressed in this book are the views of the author
and not necessarily those of The Wesleyan Church.

You will not – nor should you – agree with everything in this series.
It is not a history text. It is a series of books of opinion based on
history. But you should not dismiss it without wrestling through
these issues and the claims of the Holy Spirit on your heart and life,
and upon the Church you love.

I pray it will renew a fire among us that will burn down our religion,
burn through racial barriers, contribute to the toppling of earthly
kingdoms built on false claims and ungodly political agendas, and
burn up our prideful self-righteousness as it roars into a flame that
cannot be contained, and bursts forth in a roaring inferno of holy
love, for the Glory of God and the eternal good of
those hungering for the holiness they may not have experienced,
but know in their hearts it must exist.
The series is written primarily in narrative form, and employs the use
of personal stories and testimonies, because that seems to be the best
way to communicate
to the generations younger than me.
– Pastor Dan

FOREWORD

It is fairly easy to find older folk who see value in the past, and sense we've lost something and want to turn the clock back. Daniel LeRoy is different than this. He sees the great value of the past but instead of wanting to go back, he wants us to go forward with it. He mines the ore from the tailings of the past to find the lasting gems and proposes taking them into the future.

Yet he understands the diamonds of the past sometimes need new settings. The good things we've lost cannot be reintroduced "as is" today exactly the way they were used in the past. People change. Generations turn over and the church changes too. Today's church is a different audience. Words can take on new meanings. A word we once used easily can become completely negative in connotation. Even in our Christmas carols. A word that once had a positive response by people can now create completely negative vibrations. To reintroduce the gems from the past often takes new words and new methods. Communication changes. Speaking styles change. Music changes. And how we approach an audience persuasively changes, too. What was once considered "persuasive preaching" can be received as shouting bullying a generation later.

Danny is able to thread this difficult needle better than anyone else I've seen. He seems to understand what is worth taking forward, what "editing" of those ideas and practices needs to take place in order to recapture them today, and how to make a new holiness church in a denomination that has largely abandoned the idea, all in a way that will connect with today's audiences of church members and semi-secular casual attendees.

I hope this book gets a wide reading. Even if you are one of the many Wesleyans who store great resentment of past abuses and extremes of the holiness movement, at least give this book a chance. Read it carefully, thoughtfully and with an open mind. Who knows? You may discover there was indeed some good in what you've come to dismiss as old-fashioned holiness legalism. You may adopt some of his ideas or all of them. You might even toss out everything here by saying, "That's not the way I'd do this." Do so if you wish. But at least ask yourself first, "So, exactly how *would* I do it?"

Keith Drury

July 1, 2023

PREFACE

The scope of this book is for the North American church. I firmly believe that it applies across all Christian cultures worldwide because I believe it is sound biblical teaching. But I have to be intellectually honest. The scope of my experience is in the North American church and so really, I can only guess how it applies in the wider context. I haven't been there at all.

All the North American denominations believe in sanctification. Sometimes, but not often, they even use the word. The truth is, all Christian discipleship material is sanctification material. It is designed to make us stronger in our relationship with God, better in our behavior, deeper in our faith, and more effective in our ministry in the world.

In the North American mainline churches, sanctification has always had a place, on paper anyway. Every orthodox Christian group believes in sanctification as a component of the salvation process. How they believe it operates and what it does in the life of the believer differs widely. Almost all perceive it to be gradual and progressive. Most believe it arrives in its fullness as dying grace. Few proclaim what the American Holiness Movement has proclaimed about it, that it is definite, that it involves a crisis experience, that it is subsequent to and separate from regeneration, that it is essential for power and purity, and that it brings victory over sin in the life of the believer. But they at least acknowledge it as

18

an ongoing work of God in the life of the believer. They just don't want to talk about it. At least not the way our old-timers did.

One of the main reasons the "holiness" message as "holiness" people proclaimed it could never gain traction outside the American Holiness Movement is because of the insistence in using inflexible in-house terminology to communicate that message. In fact, that was one of the identifying factors within the movement as to whether someone was legitimate. Do they talk like us?

This pushed away others, who otherwise most likely would have been not just sympathizers, but likely advocates of the message.

That same dynamic exists even to this day. Those who self-identify as part of today's Conservative Holiness Movement point at two major divergences the other American Holiness Movement denominations have taken off the "holiness" path, in their opinion – how we dress and what terms we use or don't use to communicate the holiness message. They see those as two points of compromise.

Be that as it may, with no desire to offend my more conservative friends, my point behind the book is, if the terms we use misrepresent or miscommunicate what we're saying when the current generation hears them, and they require constant explanation every time we use them, then it's our responsibility to find better ways to say what we're trying to say. We'll see how close I can come to achieving that. It might just work. Or I might further confuse everybody. That wouldn't be the first time that's been done among us.

One of the works of the Holy Spirit is to illuminate us, to bring light to our darkened understanding. I will pray for that grace to operate in me as I write and in you as you read.

My old preacher friend J. Percy Trueblood, known as "The Walking Bible" because of the enormous amounts of scripture he had committed to memory, was a giant in the holiness ranks in the mid-Twentieth Century, preaching extensively on the camp meeting circuit and in local church revivals all over North America. He was the real thing, and had the Airstream trailer to prove it. He was from the little farming community of Bagley Swamp, tucked away in the northeast corner of North Carolina, and I got to be his pastor in the closing days of his life. Mr. Percy would often say, "What we need is some good old Holy Ghost eye salve!" That anointing to which he referred will help us see what is of the Lord and what is not, in these pages.

Let's ask our Helper and Guide to apply his holy eye salve to our eyes so we can see the way forward clearly, so we can share the message clearly.

INTRODUCTION

This is not a deep theological treatise or formal theological treatment on the doctrine of sanctification. This is a popular attempt to bring the reality of sanctifying grace back into the conversation, back into the pulpits, and back into the lives of the people of The Wesleyan Church. It has never truly, fully left. We still believe it and it is clearly in our directing and foundational documents. It still resides in our older generations. We still teach it in our schools of religion and our seminary. Our pastors believe it and live it, and swear allegiance to it in their ordination vows. But it does not get clearly proclaimed from our pulpits. Most of our preaching these days seems to be of the self-help variety, a focus on coping with the difficulties of life and how to navigate our challenging circumstances.

We hear a lot about sin, acknowledging its presence and activity around us and in us. Like President Calvin Coolidge reported about his pastor's opinion of sin, "He was ag'in it," so we know we're against it. And we're not supposed to do it. But little seems to be said directly about victory over the domination of sin in our lives, and how that is accomplished in our daily Christian walk. Much is said about sinning in word, thought and deed daily. Little is said about the overcoming power of holy love available to us in the presence and power of the Holy Spirit.

Right now, it seems to me that we have entered into a phase where "holiness" resides in our intuition and still informs our conduct and behavior from somewhere in the back of our minds, but it has moved out of the "intentional" phase of our common life as a church. It's still there. It's still influencing us. But it is far from being the driving force of our movement. It's hanging around on the margins and may fade away with the next generation.

So how do we fan this spiritual dynamic back into flame among us? We start by beginning to talk openly about it with our people again. And we talk to them in terms they can understand and in claims they can believe. We fully embrace the fire, and through the active grace burning in us, we use our influence with them to set their hearts ablaze. In order to explain to them what we are talking about and to encourage them to experience it, we would do well to redefine our holiness heritage for them. That is the purpose of this book. Find a new way to say an old but vibrant truth.

That calls for a conversation about language. In some places terms need to be refined, in other places terms need to be redefined, and in other places terms need to be replaced. Not to be novel, but to be heard.

This is not an attempt to take us back to our past. This is an attempt to bring what was real in our past back to our future.

This is not an attempt to replace the influence of the Evangelical Movement in The Wesleyan Church and erode the blessings that Movement has brought to our Wesleyan culture. This is an attempt to build on those blessings and take us beyond what "Evangelical" has to offer us.

By way of explanation, I am trying to redefine the concepts in a way that younger persons don't get tripped up by the language or

22

defensive about what they consider exaggerated or arrogant, unrealistic claims.

So this is a treatment of the doctrine of sanctification from a relational and dynamic point of view. Some old-timers will claim it is closer to Keswick than American Holiness Movement. I think it's closer to scripture, myself.

As for archaic or awkward or exaggerated terms, they are like all explanatory terms. In their day, they may have been directly on target to a point, but when pushed to logical extremes they end up being used to make claims that are not true. That fact is the truth of all human language. It is inadequate to communicate the glories of the things we experience, but it's all we have.

It is interesting to me that others outside the American Holiness Movement have found ways to communicate the holiness message in an attractive, reasonable and compelling manner.

When I was an active pastor in The Wesleyan Church, from the mid-1970s through the 1990s, when our transition from being a "Holiness" church into becoming an "Evangelical" church was in full-swing, had crested the peak and was well on the downhill side across those decades, I observed the mainstream of the Evangelical Movement picking up the holiness message we laid down. The message we were walking away from was being championed by others.

One of the best holiness books I ever read was *Loving God* by Chuck Colson. It's been a long time since I read it and I don't remember if the actual word "sanctification" ever appeared in the text, but the whole book was about how the love of God filling a person's heart finds its way out in redeeming fashion in the lives of others.

In 1977, Jerry Bridges, a Navigators team member, released *Pursuing Holiness* through NavPress. It is not rooted in the American Holiness Movement but is a convicting treatment of the subject. It is strong on its emphasis on the imputed righteousness of God, our status in Christ, but a whole generation of those otherwise untouched by the holiness message were exposed also to the truth of the imparted righteousness of God, Christ in us, and challenged to live in that reality.

R.C. Sproul was a thorough-going Calvinist advocate who was miles away from anything resembling the American Holiness Movement theologically, yet some of his most consequential contributions to the North American church were in the areas of the holiness of God and the corresponding impact of that upon the daily life of the Christian.

In 1996 at the Promise Keepers Pastors Gathering in the Georgia Dome in Atlanta, 40,000 pastors from all over North America heard Southern Baptist pastor and author Henry Blackaby preach a holiness sermon, terminology and all, that could have been preached from the platform of any holiness camp meeting in America.

Bill Bright is not a product of the American Holiness Movement either, but his tract, "Have You Made the Wonderful Discovery of the Spirit-Filled Life?" has been placed into the hands of untold thousands of people through the ministries of Campus Crusade for Christ (now CRU) and The Billy Graham Evangelistic Association.

While these authors would not have agreed with nor accepted the basic tenets of holiness theology as taught within the ranks of the American Holiness Movement, and may have at times directed criticism at that theological position, in their hearts and minds there was an awareness of "something more" out there beyond justification – a rich, refreshing and largely unexplored territory of

24

victory in Jesus that too many were not experiencing or were even aware existed. Would we like the way they said it or the terminology they were using? I am certain we felt we could say it better. But when we weren't saying it, they were.

To take a page from a holiness advocate of another generation, D.L. Moody, I would go to school on his conversation with a critic about the way Moody did evangelism. When Moody asked the man how he did evangelism, the man responded that he didn't do evangelism. "It is clear you don't like my way of doing evangelism. You raise some good points. Frankly, sometimes I do not like my way of doing evangelism. But I like my way of doing it better than your way of not doing it," Moody replied.

Maybe we do not always like the way people present the holiness message, and have good reason for our criticism. But even though I cringe sometimes, I have to like their way of saying it better than our way of not saying it.

For goodness sake, let's find a way to say it.

PART ONE

REINVENTING THE WESLEYAN CHURCH

How do we bring what was real from our past back to our future?

CHAPTER ONE

WHY WE NEED TO REINVENT
THE WESLEYAN CHURCH

It is no surprise to anyone who knows us, we Methodist types seem to have some sort of need to reinvent our churches every thirty, forty or fifty years.

The fact is, this whole enterprise started out as a reinvention. Early in his ministry, set ablaze by his encounter with God at Aldersgate, John Wesley preached the gospel everywhere they would let him into the pulpit. He preached with such fervor and conviction, he began to make his Anglican brothers and sisters uneasy. Pulpits began to close to him and preaching opportunities dried up.

At the same time, his old Holy Club friend George Whitefield had taken the gospel outside the four walls of the church and was preaching in the open air to whatever crowds would gather. The result was that people who did not feel welcome in church were responding to the Good News in droves. A revival was stirring among the poor in England.

He tried to convince his friend John Wesley to join him. This was Wesley's reaction:

I could scarce reconcile myself to this strange way of
preaching in the fields, of which he set me an example on
Sunday; having been all my life till very lately so
tenacious of every point relating to decency and order,
that I should have thought the saving of souls almost a sin
if it had not been done in a church.

Of course, Wesley did reconcile himself to it as an effective means
of reaching unreached people for Christ, saw great response from
this whole segment of the population, developed a systematic
approach of societies and classes and bands to preserve the work, led
what became the Wesleyan Revival in England, and we and all our
Methodist cousins are the rest of the story. We began as a
reinvention of the way church was being done in Eighteenth Century
England.

And the reinvention spirit spread.

Francis Asbury arrived in the Colonies in 1771, and began his
ministry assignment. He immediately set out reinventing British
Methodism to fit the demands of the rugged, less-than-genteel, and
challenging North American culture. He started in the main
northeastern cities, but when he moved out into the rural landscape,
what worked in the cities did not work so well among the scattered
population of the American frontier. So he created a new approach
for Methodist ministry — the mobile and flexible itinerancy. Thus
was born the famous Methodist circuit rider.

At the Christmas Conference in Baltimore in 1784, the Methodist
Episcopal Church in America was established. For the first time, the
Methodist movement became a Church. Asbury and Thomas Coke
were consecrated as the first bishops. Preachers were ordained. A
Book of Discipline and a *Book of Worship* were approved. Up and
down the eastern seaboard, and reaching into the interior settlements

28

and isolated areas, local churches and preaching points were organized into circuits and served by circuit riding preachers anywhere people lived. The Methodist Church flourished in population centers and rural areas as well, because the Methodists were entrepreneurial geniuses at reinventing themselves, adapting their methods to fit their varying situations.

Some thirty years later, the American phenomenon of the Camp Meeting emerged and the Methodists adopted it as a major part of their ministry strategy. Groups of local churches banded together to establish and support local camp meeting ministries and properties. At the same time, the churches and preachers were agitating for preachers to "locate" in specific parishes, as opposed to Asbury's strong preference for the circuit riding model. The result was that by the time of his passing in 1814, local churches with appointed pastors had become the preferred model of ministry. The Methodist Church had reinvented itself into becoming a settled denomination as opposed to a movement.

The next major reinvention occurred some thirty years later when the tensions in the North American culture were beginning to boil over. In 1842, five preachers and their churches separated from the Methodist Church over the issues of slavery and episcopal abuse of power to form the Wesleyan Methodist Connection. In 1845, as the same pressures continued to build, threatening to rip apart the nation, the whole Methodist denomination splintered into three separate groups, the Methodist Episcopal Church, the Methodist Episcopal Church-South, and the Methodist Protestant Church.

Some fifty years later, the Bishops of the Methodist Episcopal Church read a letter to the General Conference of 1896, disassociating themselves as a denomination from the American Holiness Movement, which had been contained within the Methodist Church since the 1830s. As a result, well over one hundred thousand people "came out" of the three Methodist denominations, to form independent holiness churches, and then holiness denominations.

About forty years later, in 1939, the three Methodist denominations decided to kiss and make up, merging into the reconstructed Methodist Church.

Then in 1968, thirty years after that merger, the Methodist Church merged with the Evangelical United Brethren to form the United Methodist Church.

Now, fifty years later, they are in the painful process of deconstructing and reconstructing again.

Their holiness children and grandchildren haven't done much better, merging then splitting then splitting again into numerous different groups over the last one hundred and twenty-five years.

There must be some imperfection somewhere in that perfectionist DNA of ours.

Yes, there is. It is us.

The Wesleyan Church has undergone a morphing over time, until now our predecessors would hardly recognize us. Besides the adaptations in worship styles and the move to respectability in the suburbs, which are not radical reinventions, there has been a fundamental shift away from our holiness roots. We are still a holiness church and we still believe the holiness doctrine, but it is not at the heart of who we are anymore.

As hard as it is to say this, we need to reinvent The Wesleyan Church. We don't need to drag The Wesleyan Church back into the past. It's gone. We couldn't go back there if we wanted to. But we do have a say in who we become as we move forward. So what would a reinvented, holiness church bearing the name of The Wesleyan Church look like? How do we set about reinventing The Wesleyan Church? How do we move forward in faith, but retain our holiness DNA, so we can bring holiness back to the heart of The Wesleyan Church?

It's one thing to talk about it philosophically. But if you review the reinvention stories referenced earlier, there was a lot of hurt and anger and unresolved resentment woven all through those processes. How do we reinvent The Wesleyan Church without maiming each other, splitting into pieces, and embarrassing God? How do we get back on track to being the church God called us to be?

I believe healthy reinvention comes through a Spirit-led redefining of our holiness heritage by redefining our way of thinking about sanctification, redefining the core foundations of our holiness faith, redefining the language we use to communicate our holiness message, redefining our goals so that love becomes the proof for us of the sanctified life, and redefining witness into a willingness to humbly tell our story to each other and anyone who will listen. That's the path.

The result would be a recovery of the sanctified life at the heart of who we are. Not a list of expected behaviors. Not a focus on power and giftedness. Not an introspective form of sin management. Not an unrealistic expectation of perfect performance. Simply a life transformed by the power of the Holy Spirit that completely shifts our focus from ourselves, to a life focused on loving God and loving the people around us, and the ones we can go to, and the ones we have to sacrifice to go to, and don't quit until God does.

We need to reinvent The Wesleyan Church.

Can we somehow get this thing turned around? Can we somehow get this right? This is a mission-minded generation. Can we somehow get beyond ourselves and realize the mission of God in the world is designed to be carried out by a Spirit-filled, Spirit-empowered, sanctified, self-sacrificing people who are willing to follow their Savior to the Cross and beyond in order to see his kingdom come, his will be done, on earth as it is in heaven?

That is the Wesleyan mission, because that is the mission of God in every time and place. To accomplish that mission requires a sanctified people.

We need to reinvent The Wesleyan Church.

So here is the question. Is it possible, by the empowering grace of God, for me to be everything God is asking me to be in this moment? And us to be everything God is asking us to be together in this moment? And The Wesleyan Church to be everything we are called to be in this moment?

Yes, it is.

It is, through humble obedience to the leading of the Holy Spirit. Moment by moment. Day by day. Correcting where correction is needed. And walking in the light with him step by step. A willingness to open our hands, release our grip, and surrender it all to him. A willingness to let him through us reinvent The Wesleyan Church.

Just begin anew with a humble walk of obedience in the direction of our holiness calling. By his grace, we can do that. We can reinvent The Wesleyan Church, for the world's good and God's glory.

CHAPTER TWO

WHAT DOES REINVENTING THE WESLEYAN CHURCH LOOK LIKE?

What if someone gave you a beautiful new house? Not necessarily big. Modest even, but beautiful and brand new. The kind of house that grabbed your heart the moment you saw it. The kind of house that would make you start dreaming of the future you could have in it. How you could raise a family in this house. How you could change this or expand that. How you could live in it in such a way that says, "I love this house! This is so me!" And others who know you would agree. "Yep, that's you!"

John Wesley used such an image (not quite so dramatically, I must admit) to communicate the concept of the sanctified life to a friend.

The image from Wesley was, repentance is the porch, justification is the door, and sanctification is the house. The implication is, if you stepped up onto the porch in repentance and entered the door through justification, are you going to live in the house of sanctification? It's a beautiful house to live in and the possibilities are as limitless as the gifts that come from the One "who is able to do immeasurably more than all we ask or imagine, according to his power that is at work within us, to him be glory in *that house* and in Christ Jesus throughout all generations, forever and ever! Amen." Ephesians 3:20-21 with a little adaptation.

33

How fully would you live in that house? How blessed would you be by that house? How would that house enrich your life?

Now is the time. We need to reinvent The Wesleyan Church. We need to reinvent The Wesleyan Church in a way that encourages our people to live fully in the house they've been given. We need to reinvent The Wesleyan Church, but unlike some of the previously mentioned reinventions, our reinvention does not need to be a deconstruction or a reconstruction. It is not in any way an organizational or even missional reinvention in nature.

It only needs to be a refocus. But it needs to be a major refocus. A fundamental refocus. Not an about-face, but an honest look back, an intense look inward and then a determined look forward. It does not need to be so much a subtraction. We don't need to stop doing anything we are doing now. It does need to be a major addition, however.

We need to find a way to put the sanctified life back at the heart of The Wesleyan Church. How do we do that in a way that it reinvents our Church?

Right now we are focused on our evangelistic mission. We are focused on our mission globally. We continue to make ministry to children and youth a major priority. We are focused on educating our young adults through a Christ-centered, trustworthy university experience that builds them into strong, contributing Christians and leaders. We are deeply invested in all it takes to raise up and deploy strong Wesleyan pastors. We even launched our own seminary. We continue to be concerned about deliberately opening the doors of opportunity for women, women in ministry and leadership, ethnic minorities, the poor, the disenfranchised, the immigrant and others who tend to get passed over or passed by. And we continue to value our living and ministering together in loving fellowship.

All of these things, and more, we should be doing. Those are all properly Wesleyan in mission and nature.

But would a Spirit-filled, sanctified Wesleyan people be better empowered to carry out these missional assignments? Would our people, hearing the holiness message and embracing it, make a more lasting and deeper impact upon the lost world in which they live? Would being filled with the Spirit not only bless them but would it not also bless the world and the kingdom, as well?

I just have to believe a reorientation in that direction by our "holiness" denomination would have to radically change The Wesleyan Church — and thus the world and eternity.

If enough of us get burdened about it and decide that this has to happen, and begin talking about it and preaching about it and praying it into existence, our Church can be a holiness church again, finding a new level of empowerment through the Spirit because our good people experience the deeper sanctifying grace God has for them.

Here's how I propose we approach this, humbly asking God to take us to a new level in our walk with him, through his sanctifying grace.

It happens through:
Regaining our bearings.
Renewing our minds.
Refreshing our language.
Refocusing on love.
Retelling our stories.

If we were to set out on this path with deliberate intention and driving purpose, and God were to bless it, we would find ourselves living in a reinvented Wesleyan Church and seeing a dramatic change everywhere we have influence. We would see what was real from our past being brought back to our future.

Back to the house illustration . . .

We each should set our heart to discover, explore and live fully in every bit of that house. It'll take a lifetime. It'll end up being a defining factor in who you are. It'll become the center of the joy and fulfillment you'll experience in relationship with God, your family, your neighbors and everyone you know. To many, it will in fact be you.

Every illustration has its limitations, but the point is, there's more. How do we help our people discover the "more"? If we can accomplish that, if we can lead our people into that kind of experience with God, we will have reinvented The Wesleyan Church.

CHAPTER THREE

WHY DID THE WESLEYAN CHURCH REINVENT ITS MEMBERSHIP STRUCTURE?

There were several theological and philosophical reasons why The Wesleyan Church changed its membership structure, but the main reason was to bring discipleship back to the heart of The Wesleyan Church. And what is discipleship essentially? It's another term for the personal process of sanctification.

We had always offered a "contra mundum" membership philosophy, first, based in John Wesley's pattern of making disciples, and, second, serving as a reaction or correction to the membership philosophies of the mainline churches. We saw their approach being closer to country club membership (pay your dues and enjoy the privileges), than the narrow gate into the kingdom. We were all about the narrow gate.

In the process of morphing into being an Evangelical Church, we found the narrow gate and narrow path to be too confining. Especially as it meant you had to travel a long way down the narrow path before we would let you through the narrow gate.

Something was backwards here.

We likened the mainline approach to following a "Belong Believe Become" path, with belonging coming before people were even "saved" (our word). We understood their approach. We just didn't agree with it.

Our path was described as "Believe Become Belong", which meant you had to master our language, lifestyle and look before we would acknowledge you were one of us. That made sense in the context of the American Holiness Movement. It made membership the reward for becoming an accomplished disciple. As noble as that was, it just didn't match up to the Bible. And our people wearied of it. It definitely made no sense to newcomers. It seemed prideful and, frankly, unbiblical to them. And they were right.

While there is no membership structure spelled out in the Book of Acts or the epistles, members of the New Testament church, by inference, met four entry requirements: a clear conversion, Christian baptism, adherence to the teachings of the Apostles, and allegiance to the local church. They belonged. They were "members". That was at the start of the path for them, not way down the path.

So we had the courage to reinvent our membership structure, moving membership to the beginning of the process instead of using it as a goal further into the process. "Believe Belong Become" is now our pattern.

But we didn't make that fundamental change just to be more in line with the New Testament, although that's enough of a reason certainly. We made the change because we realized that over time we had let the discipleship mission of the church get away from us. It was a fundamental missional change.

The greatest contributor to the shift away from a strong discipleship mission was the demise of the Sunday school. We quit doing that in a lot of places, and it has dwindled in others. But we never came up with a serious discipleship strategy to replace it. Basically, once you got past youth group you were on your own, structurally, and we hoped you were getting it in the worship service.

In reinventing the membership structure we reemphasized the discipleship mission. We rewrote *The Discipline* to codify the change. It is back at the heart of who we are.

Now the pulpit and the discipleship resources give us a platform for helping our people understand, embrace, experience and share the beautiful reality of the sanctifying grace of God in their lives. If we now have the courage to talk about it.

Pastors and leaders, if we will buy into the shift and put the message of sanctification back at the center of our lives, our preaching, our teaching — that is how we reinvent The Wesleyan Church.

CHAPTER FOUR

REINVENTING THE CHURCH AND TRASHING OUR TRADITION ARE NOT THE SAME THING

Trashing tradition seems to be *en vogue* these days.

Tradition is suspicious to some of us. Of little value in a practical way. Largely irrelevant. Insignificant to making any meaningful contribution to the realities of today.

It is of importance to those who lived it. Not so much to those who've only heard about it.

The old-timers lacked the sophistication of our day. They did not have the breadth of world knowledge we have. Or, for most, the level of education with which we have been blessed.

If you listen to some folks today, you might even think our ancestors were all idiots.

Well, they weren't.

What they lacked in sophistication or formal schooling, they made up for with their intelligence, their wisdom and their clean living, as holiness people. And truthfully, many of the leaders did have advanced degrees.

For us to trash our tradition just because it is tradition is infantile. It's like children who do not understand that it is the contribution of their great-grandparents, grandparents and parents that has put them where they are. And in their limited perspective, what is important to them and their generation right now is all that is important.

That is a very short-sighted and impoverished way to live your life.

In the Wesleyan thought process, tradition has always held a place of great honor. It's how we remember who we are. It's how we trace our Wesleyan DNA to our ancestral roots. It is how we have always gauged our fidelity to our values and our authenticity as a movement. It's how we measure our character. It's how we remember our history. And it's an agent in our growth in grace.

Our tradition flows out of scripture, as understood and taught by our spiritual grandfather, John Wesley, and was passed on to us through the American Holiness Movement. It is "the faith once delivered to the saints," run through the Wesleyan-Arminian cognitive grid, and lived out in the real world as a witness to the even more real world that we cannot see but to which we bow.

It is an anchor for our souls. And anchors are very important in stormy times.

Tradition runs counter to a worldview that assumes only what is happening now has value. For those who do not understand its place and value, tradition gets sacrificed on the altar of immediate practicality.

41

That's a problem for Wesleyans. We are not primarily practical people. We are primarily principled people. And instead of sacrificing our principles in order to be practical, we sacrifice ourselves in order to be aligned with the holy will of God, even when it puts us in uncomfortable positions with our friends. We understand that submission to his will is the pathway of our sanctification. And that sanctification is expressed in how we live. And how we live reflects the expectations of scripture. And scriptural expectations can be identified and honored — both in our actions and our attitudes. The work of God in our lives should always be evidenced by the way we live our lives.

Our adherence to those expectations does not sanctify us. Only God can do that. It is his sanctifying grace working in us that produces those actions and attitudes in us, which are then expressed outward from us.

In times of temptation. In times of honor. In times of peaceful idleness. In times of turbulence. In all times, at all times, the sanctifying power of the Holy Spirit works in and through us to help us love God with all we are, and love our neighbor as we want to be loved.

That spirit of submission is also the avenue of blessing. And the blessing of God more than makes up for our crafty practicalities that we think win us favor with people we are trying to reach. It is the anointing that attracts them to Jesus through us, not our human accommodations. And where our craftiness falls short, and it always will, it is the anointing of God that adds dimensions of depth and power and effectiveness to our ministry we could never even imagine, let alone manufacture. The older generations understood this. Those who honor God receive honor from God. That's what they lived for.

Granted, they did not always get it right. And we have modified their list of expected behaviors multiple times across the decades. But what they did get right is that there is a life, unpolluted by the unhelpful influences of the world, powered by the personal presence of God the Holy Spirit in our lives, that bears a clear and compelling witness to those captivated by sin that there is a better Way.

But they won't believe it if they don't see it. And they won't see it if we don't live it. Throwing out our "tradition" of careful living and joining them in sins that captivate them is definitely not what they need from us.

We've done some "not so bright" things at times in our history. Uncritically trashing our tradition might just be close to the top of the list. What we want, actually, is to experience what was real in the lives of those old-timers, in the context of our day. There are some traditions that have to go if we are actually going to experience that. But there are some that are rooted in scripture, good sense and godly experience that will prove to bring us closer to God and be a word of good news to our neighbors.

Our experience should teach us that following tradition for tradition's sake is akin to idolatry, but trashing tradition uncritically might just be the fruit of spiritual pride. A Spirit-led reinvention of The Wesleyan Church will have room for old treasures among the new.

PART TWO

RENEWING OUR MINDS

How do we change our way of thinking about holiness in ways
that will help our emerging generations get over all the negative
impressions they got from the older generations,
and from our poor example?

CHAPTER FIVE

SEVEN GUIDING PRINCIPLES FOR RENEWING THE WAY WE THINK ABOUT OUR HOLINESS HERITAGE

How can we lead our people, especially our younger people, to experience the deeper grace of the sanctified life, that will bless them, make a measurable difference in the world, and help The Wesleyan Church get back what we gave away? How can we adjust our thinking so that we can find our way back home?

At this point you might expect a step-by-step diagram for a pathway into the life of holiness. No. That's a major part of what got us into trouble before – trying to reduce a dynamic relationship with God into a workable, controllable human formula. Relationships and formulas do not tend to work well together in the fluid dynamics of the real world.

In working through the process of finding our way back, there are seven principles (not steps) that I would propose following, like one would follow a compass, to help us avoid the mistakes of the past, that together become a "true north" guide for the path forward. These seven foundational principles form the cognitive grid through which all my thinking on this matter passes. You may not always see them expressed in this form, but you should hear the echo of them throughout the contents of this book, and this "Our Holiness Heritage" series. This is the philosophical, and I believe biblical, foundation upon which this appeal to bring holiness back to the heart of The Wesleyan Church is built.

I offer these guiding principles that I believe will take us in the right direction:

Principle 1:

Apologies and Repentance

I believe we should make a sincere and sorrow-filled apology to our past generations and our emerging generations for messing this up.

> I attempt to apologize for what I and my friends did to The Wesleyan Church in the next chapter. I won't presume to apologize for you and your friends.

Principle 2:

Relational and Dynamic

I believe we should reinforce the transition from the use of inflexible formulas and proof-texting arguments to relational and dynamic terms and concepts, marked most clearly by holy love.

> The generations preceding us came up in an era when propositional truth reigned. This was the way they understood and communicated the "doctrine of sanctification." To them sanctification was more of a religious idea with less emphasis on the relational reality. This is in spite of the fact that their hero, John Wesley, clearly and boldly proclaimed, "The Gospel of Christ knows of no religion but social; no holiness, but social holiness."

> In our day, this concept has been twisted to support what is known as "the social gospel" by liberals seeking to claim an endorsement from Wesley for their understanding. That is not what Wesley meant. The statement is made in the preface

47

to a book of hymns, *Hymns and Sacred Poems* published for the societies in 1739, to be used in corporate worship, and his meaning is that true Christian experience takes place in community, through sanctified relationships.

"Social religion" is loving God with all your heart, soul, mind, and strength, and "social holiness" is loving your neighbor as yourself.

Therefore, a proper understanding of sanctification is that it is not so much a state of religious attainment, but it is relational and dynamic in nature.

Principle 3:
Recognizable and Understandable
I believe we should redefine traditional and mostly abandoned holiness terms and concepts into terms and concepts that are recognizable and understandable by the emerging generation in the church today.

I believe we must engage the rising generation using language they understand and will receive.

Terms and verbiage that communicated well to other generations are not sacred. Words and phrases are tools. We should then speak about this beautiful, dynamic relationship in a way this generation will understand it, embrace it, experience it, be transformed by it, and in turn be able and motivated to share it.

We cannot let the vocabulary get in the way of the message.

Principle 4:
Reasonable and Desirable
I believe we should speak in terms of reasonable and desirable outcomes that are outgrowths of "the fruit of the Spirit" rather than forming lists of expected behaviors.

Make love the proof.

Previous generations had a tendency to make performance the proof. So we ended up with long lists of expected and required behaviors, which were well-meaning, but led too often to people serving the list rather than living the true life. That led to legalism, and legalism kills true life.

For some, the proof was in power. So we ended up in some places with some pretty strange activity that was claimed to be the work of the Holy Spirit. It may have been, or it may not have been. But it seldom seemed to lead to more love. And it too often led to a spiritual lust for more exhibitions and, unfortunately, exhibitionism.

For some, the proof of the sanctified life was in the gifts. And certain gifts became elevated in value and desire above other gifts. This led to some unfortunate claims of exclusion if a person did not happen to receive the special gift or gifts a group thought they should receive to be legitimately sanctified.

I believe we should go back to Wesley (and Jesus and Paul and John), and make love the proof of the sanctified life.

Principle 5:

Optimistic and Compelling

I believe we should major on optimistic grace, and minimize the negative, especially legalism and a judgmental spirit.

Too many in our past seemed to prefer austere and intimidating over optimistic and compelling. That was also an unfortunate mistake that caused later generations to walk away.

I even remember conversation about deathbed repentance where the more austere folks seemed to exhibit an attitude of resentment that such a thing could happen. It was almost as though they felt cheated that they had to live such a strict life all this time, and these latecomers were going to skate home scot-free?

The truth is, they themselves did not have to live such a sour life. It was self-imposed or imposed by other sour-heads upon them. They completely missed the joy of the Lord that was available to them, and is so attractive to others. I'm not sure what they had, and I have every confidence they made it to heaven. But they did not exhibit the life marked by being filled with holy love and joy that was available to them.

If they made it, I hope they are enjoying themselves now.

Principle 6:

True to the Bible and True to life.

I believe we should avoid the unfortunate tendency of too many in the past to claim unrealistic and unbiblical characteristics and expectations as indicators of the sanctified life.

The preachers were trying their best to communicate what they sincerely believed the Bible taught about the life of sanctification, but there was a major disconnect between what they were preaching and what they and the people in the pew were experiencing.

The pastors knew the language and the phrasing. They had the head knowledge regarding the doctrine. A favorite pastime of holiness preachers was to sit under the shade of the trees during camp meeting and discuss and debate the finer points of holiness theology. They were immersed in it. But the practical points were too often dismissed or ignored. The tendency seemed to be, when challenged that this wasn't working like they claimed it worked, instead of entering into sensitive and caring conversation, they instead took to the pulpit and doubled down on the claims.

What people were hearing and what people were experiencing were not matching up. That was a practical problem that grew into a credibility problem that resulted eventually in people dismissing the not-true-to-life claims of the preachers.

This is sanctification we are talking about here, not glorification. It's a tragic mistake to get the two mixed up.

Principle 7:
Honest and Meaningful
I believe we should have the courage and good sense to ask and honestly answer the question, does it really even matter anymore? And if it does, what are we going to do about it?

We talk about things that matter to us, don't we?

Are we hearing any conversations among our people about the joy and peace they are experiencing because of being completely "sold out" to Christ? Is the sanctified life being talked about from our pulpits and in our small groups? Are our people sharing with other believers their experience of a deeper life beyond "being saved"? Is there more to our preaching and their experience beyond justification?

Does it matter?

When it matters again to our people, that will be the sign that we have brought holiness back to the heart of The Wesleyan Church.

Perhaps we need to think and talk less in static terms and more in dynamic terms when we are talking about our spiritual growth. We need to think less in terms of stages and more in terms of dynamic and growing relationships.

Our spiritual life should be like the stock market in a healthy economy. There will be peaks and there may be plunges, but across the long view there should be a dynamic, detectable, even measurable growth upward. I like to refer to this pattern as the work of the Holy Spirit in us making us more and more like Christ and less and less like the person we used to be.

Instead of saying, "I am sanctified," we should probably acknowledge the Spirit's ongoing, never ending work in us by humbly saying instead, "I am being sanctified." Not only has God done a sanctifying work in us, but that work continues on.

Apologies and repentance
Relational and dynamic
Recognizable and understandable

Reasonable and desirable
Optimistic and compelling
True to the Bible and true to life
Honest and meaningful

These are the guiding principles that will inform and direct our
conversation as we explore the process of renewing our minds in
how we understand the work of God in sanctification. They are
relational and dynamic in nature, as opposed to the static
terminology and concepts that have characterized so many of our
conversations in the past. By following these principles, hopefully
we will help our emerging generation do what they do best – talk to
each other – in the way they learn best – by narrative – and so
recover such things from our past as the clear assurance of the
sanctifying work in a person's life, the embrace of that experience,
the joy of deep-settled peace with God that spills over into the world
that is anything but peace-filled, and the testimony that compels
others to explore the possibility that they too could possibly
experience the same thing in their lives because they know there has
to be more to it than what they are experiencing.

While different in form and phrasing, I believe I hear the echo of the
principles that fueled the Wesleyan Revival and the American
Holiness Movement for decades.

By the renewing of our minds through the tender grace and mercy of
the Holy Spirit, let's get back to the dynamics of holy love. Let's
refresh our language. Let's cultivate the fruit of the Spirit. Let's
rejoice in optimistic grace. Let's make good sense rooted in
scriptural wisdom. Let's help our emerging generation understand
why it matters.

By the renewing of our minds through the tender grace and mercy of
the Holy Spirit, let's get back to being holiness Wesleyans.

CHAPTER SIX

MY APOLOGY FOR WHAT MY FRIENDS AND I DID TO THE WESLEYAN CHURCH

We were handed a beautiful, attainable expression of Jesus' promise of abundant life, and in many places, that wonderful experience thrived in the lives of our people. But in too many places, we shrunk it down to where we could manage it without his help, and then we threw it to the side and walked away from it. What some were claiming to be "Bible holiness" wasn't living up to those claims, it wasn't making a transformational difference in our lives, and it wasn't anything anyone would stand in line to get. It was just religion with rules and expectations but no life. We should apologize and repent with godly sorrow.

When the American Holiness Movement began to calcify into institutions – local churches, denominations, colleges and Bible Schools – as all human institutions tend to do, we gradually drifted into the cooling down phase and the organizational phase and the "keeping of the traditions" phase, until it became all too rare to encounter the dynamic fire that once was so characteristic of the "Movement." We defined it. We explained it. We intellectually bisected it. We codified it. We reduced it to a formula, and a list of expected behaviors. We dived deep into the minutia, and neglected (if I may paraphrase Jesus) the weightier matters of the grace. The first we should have done, without neglecting the latter. In fact, we stopped talking about sanctifying grace, and only talked about sanctification.

We moved from dynamic to static language, and from vibrant experience in our hearts and lives to technical expression on paper.

We could teach it and discuss it and debate it with the best of them. Living in the fullness of the promise was another matter altogether.

We did what everybody does. We walked away from the mystery and moved to the mechanical. We traded the experience for the explanation. Instead of the demonstration, we became content with the definition. We took that which was real and reduced it to a two-step formula. We gravitated to that which we could mimic. We had haughtily disdained the Catholics and their "bells and smells" but, in way too many places, we instituted our own human efforts and behavioral expectations and requirements, leaving the impression that by looking a certain way and behaving a certain way, we could make ourselves holy. We knew better, but we didn't do better. Don't you know our self-righteousness must have been a stench in the nostrils of our holy, loving God? In too many places, we substituted human holiness in place of the sanctifying power of the Holy Spirit. Moses with a bag over his head would have felt at home in too many Wesleyan churches. The glory had departed in too many places, but we still looked and talked the holiness part. And our younger generation departed, not from the church, but from the teaching, because they found too little authenticity in our claims or our lives.

The heart of the matter is that we drifted away from our holiness heritage and settled for a safe, respectable expression of Evangelical Christianity.

My generation did that. We weren't happy with our experience in the "Holiness Movement." We were embarrassed by it, sadly. And we were drawn to the "Evangelical Movement," content to be a subset of that more respectable (we thought) group of North American Christians. It felt good to be part of a group that was getting attention for the right reasons for once. As a result, my generation did not preach a clear message of holiness from our pulpits. We still believed in it and experienced it. We passed our ordination examinations, well able to answer the question, "How do you understand the Wesleyan distinctive of sanctification?" When it came to proclaiming it, though, we tried to find every way we could to say it without saying it. The word "sanctification" virtually disappeared from our vocabulary. If we talked about it at all, we preferred to use the word "holiness" but we did not get into the demonstration of the life or the invitation into the life. We just acknowledged it, and moved on. We eventually focused on evangelism and Spirit-filled worship, and left sanctification in the rear-view mirror. One of the sad, unintended consequences of that set of decisions was that deliberate discipleship also got left in the rear-view mirror. Sunday School pretty much died away, and the mission of discipleship pretty much dried up among us.

With the strategic reformatting of our membership structure, moving Membership from the end of the line – Believe, Become, Belong – toward the front of the line – Believe, Belong, Become – discipleship has been given a renewed life. It is intentional and effective now, like it used to be. Since that is the core of The Great Commission we received from the Lord himself, it is a very good thing that we have undone our tragic mistake and got things back in order of priority again.

But with sanctification, my generation messed that up. We owe a direct, sincere and heartfelt apology in two directions.

First, we owe an apology to the people who handed us the Church, fully expecting we would take care of it and be worthy of their trust. We were not. For what appears to be selfish reasons from where we sit today, we gave it away. After all their struggles, all their studies, all their sacrifices, all their sanctified impact on a less-than sanctified world, we decided to take a different path. My generation did that. Orange, Luther, Jotham, LaRoy and Lucius, I'm sorry. My hero, Adam, I'm sorry. Seth and Martin, I'm sorry. Raymond, you took me under your care and shepherded me, signing my ordination certificate, and I let you down. I'm so sorry. To all those who entrusted us with this "Grand Depositum," we let you down and I am sorry. I repent with tears.

Second, we owe an apology to those who are coming behind us. There were those who faked it and falsified it, giving insincere testimony and making outlandish claims, loading people down with unbearable burdens and unrealistic demands. And there were those of us who knew people – our parents, our grandparents, our pastors, our leaders – who without doubt lived in the fullness of holiness and their lives proved it, their love excelled, and their faces shined, yet we were embarrassed by the other crowd, and instead of championing the real thing, we bailed. We took what looked like an appropriate exit from the bumpy old Highway of Holiness onto the broader and smoother, more scenic Speedway of Evangelicalism. We still had the "Holiness Unto the Lord" bumper sticker on the car, but we preferred the "Moral Majority" license plate on the front bumper.

Have you ever heard of buyer's remorse?

Decades later, we have passed on to our children and grandchildren, and their friends, a shallow faith that costs very little, and is suspect as to whether it will stand up against what is coming. What have we done? When this time calls for a robust faith and holy life, what have

57

we handed to them? I am sorry Peyton, Raegan, Anna Grace, Elboy, Luke, Sam, Owen, Ainsley and Nellie. As your grandfather, I pray that your church will preach to you the whole gospel, and will intentionally and consistently, with conviction, invite you to go deeper in your walk with the Lord. I pray that you find yourselves in a church under the loving care of a pastor who will call you to the kind of sanctifying faith and holy life the church at Antioch was challenged by Barnabas to embrace:

"When he arrived and saw what the grace of God had done, he was glad and encouraged them all to remain true to the Lord with all their hearts." - Acts 11:23

PART THREE

REFRESHING OUR LANGUAGE

How do we give the emerging generations a new and compelling
way to understand, embrace, experience and share
the deeper grace of the sanctified life?

CHAPTER SEVEN

WHY WE NEED TO REFRESH OUR HOLINESS LANGUAGE

Too much of our sanctification language has been mechanical and formulaic, failing to be true to the Bible and true to life. We need to refresh our vocabulary, making sure it is relational and dynamic in nature. We need to be able to communicate this beautiful concept in a way that the emerging generation will understand it, embrace it, experience it, and be able to share it.

For example:

When we want to talk about "holiness," what do our younger people hear? If it is a tainted term to them, because of excesses and poor representations, why don't we talk about becoming more and more like Christ and less and less like the person we used to be?

When we want to talk about "being holy," what does that mean to a younger person? Why don't we help them understand it by talking about being Christlike?

When we want to talk about "entire sanctification," younger people tend to hear that as an arrogant claim of spiritual superiority. Maybe we should use the scriptural phrase, being sanctified through and through, instead.

When we want to talk about "consecration," why don't we use their term, going all in?

When we want to talk about "surrendering to the will of God," why don't we talk about that as learning to say "yes" to God?

When we want to talk about "heart purity," why don't we talk in terms of integrity and faithfulness and trustworthiness?

"Eradication" was one of the terms used for a while in the holiness movement, but it fell out of favor. Maybe instead we could talk about the deep conversion of our souls?

Instead of talking about "second blessing holiness," why don't we talk about seeking everything God has for us, no matter how many blessings it involves?

Instead of talking about a "second definite work of grace subsequent to regeneration," why don't we just talk about seeking everything God has next for us?

When we use the term "sanctification," why don't we add the positive dimension of grace to it – sanctifying grace?

When we want to talk about "being filled with the Spirit," why don't we explain it as the very Presence of God himself living in us? Instead of talking about "being filled with power," why don't we talk about having everything we need to be everything we're supposed to be?

"Christian perfection" has been one of the more misunderstood and misrepresented phrases used in holiness terminology. Why don't we just talk about growing in spiritual maturity?

61

Instead of talking about "original sin," why don't we talk about being broken way down deep?

Instead of talking about having "the victory," why don't we talk about being given the ability not to be dominated by sin?

We need to maintain the technical language of our holiness theology in the textbooks and in the commentaries and in the classroom, but we need to change our language in our preaching and in our testifying and in our conversations.

Too many of us don't talk about it because the language gets in the way.

Allow me to say again, we have to talk to this generation in a vocabulary they understand and will receive. Terms that communicated to earlier generations are not sacred. Words and phrases are tools. We need, then, to speak about this basic, beautiful truth in a way this generation will understand, embrace, and experience it. We desire to see their lives be transformed by it, and in turn see them be able and motivated to share it. But we can't let the vocabulary get in the way of the message.

CHAPTER EIGHT

ORIGINAL SIN

"Original sin" is the theological concept that following the fall of Adam into sin, every person born since then – with the exception of Jesus of Nazareth – is born into a broken relationship with God.

While understanding the technical aspects of original sin is a critical piece of theological knowledge, finding a way to communicate the concept in narrative form may be more effective with the rising generation. The narrative might look like this:

For me, this matter of being broken way down deep inside, what the theologians call original sin, has a name. I call it Old Dan.

Old Dan gives me more trouble than anyone I know. He is a nasty old buzzard that lives somewhere in the regions of my being that Richard Taylor, Twentieth Century spokesperson for the American Holiness Movement, identified as "deeper down and further back." Taylor was a preacher and professor in The Church of The Nazarene, and a prolific writer. My friend, Darius Salter, a renowned preacher, teacher and writer himself in that tribe, and influencer in the American Holiness Movement, says by his count Taylor authored more than twenty-five books. While he was prolific, he was not a degreed or certified psychologist or psychiatrist. But he knew human nature.

There is something deep inside each of us that is broken and untamed, that none of us can fully understand or comprehend. It is a power. It is an influence. It is an orientation away from God and focused on self. From atheist Sigmund Freud on one end of the scale all the way to holiness developmental theorist Donald Joy on the other – no matter how we may try to dig deep into the abyss, we will never this side of heaven fully understand or explain the "deeper down and further back."

Old Dan lives down there.

And just when me and Jesus have our good thing going, Old Dan pops up and creates all manner of mischief. Crouching at the door, he catches me distracted and when I'm not looking, he jumps into the driver's seat and grabs the wheel. A lot of times, before I even know it, he has steered us off the highway and into the ditch. So far he hasn't driven us off a cliff, but it's not because he hasn't tried. I find myself riding with Carrie Underwood on those occasions, screaming for Jesus to take the wheel! And he does.

What can I do with Old Dan? The old timers in the American Holiness Movement were strong on preaching the crucifixion of the Old Man. Well, I must be doing it wrong, because I've driven every kind of nail I can find into that Old Dan. I've driven stakes into his heart and more than once riddled his carcass with silver bullets. That old buzzard just won't die.

Now don't get me wrong. He does not dominate my life anymore. He does not have free rein in my life. God in his grace has drawn a line in my life that Old Dan is not allowed to cross. And God in his grace has interposed the power of the shed blood of Jesus Christ as a barrier that keeps Old Dan in bounds. And God in his grace has come to live in my life through his Holy Spirit in a way that keeps Old Dan at bay.

But he still prowls around. He still sneaks in and messes with things. He still fans the flame of pride and arrogance in me, trying his best to burn my life down. He stills jumps at every opportunity to derail me through what I see or what I hear or what I think or what I do.

Old Dan has an uncanny ability in my life to know how to effectively mess with me.

I've always been a person who is easy to get along with. I was a compliant child. I was such a good child, my parents were convinced they were the Perfect Parents (until my sister came along). My path in life has been relatively straight and smooth, and I have never gone completely off the track. The worst thing I did as a child was tell my eight year old neighbor there wasn't any Santa Claus. I have never smoked a cigarette. I have never had a drink of beer (although I have had a drink of wine a couple of times when taking communion in an Episcopal Church). I don't cheat. I am faithful to my wife. I don't lie. (I did pause to convince myself that was not a lie as I wrote it, then hurried on.) I haven't murdered anyone. I have honored my parents. I am careful how I conduct myself on Sunday. You can trust me with money. And I am proud not to be proud.

See what I mean? Proud Old Dan wrote all of that.

So, for me the question at this point becomes, what can we authentically claim that the grace of God in sanctification can do for or with Old Dan?

To put the question as the old-timers wrestled with it, in their terms of understanding, how does the grace of God in sanctification address the reality and dynamic of Original Sin in the life of a believer?

This current generation may be tempted to ask their own question, echoing the vast majority of the Church across the ages who refused to deal with it – "Who cares? That's way beyond my pay grade and outside my areas of concern. I just want to know how to get to Heaven."

Is there a life for me not dominated by Old Dan? Yes, there is.

Is this a message that will preach to our people? Is this a message our people need to hear? Is this a truth that will prick their curiosity about the depth of their walk with God and the health of their relationships with others? Is this something that, when they hear it, they will be inclined to say, "I have wondered if such a thing could be true and I am really interested in finding out more"? Is the message of John Wesley a message for today? Is the message of Jesus and Paul and John a message for today? Is there a market for a holistic presentation of the Gospel that moves beyond the fire escape mentality of too many shallow Christians and the behavioral checklist mentality of many legalists in the American Holiness Movement, and appeals to the depth of hunger for a right and fulfilling relationship with God and the others in their lives in this day?

In all that is wrong all around us, and inside us, is there an innate hunger for the truly optimistic grace that is offered in the holiness message when it is properly understood and communicated and lived out?

For every Old Dan wreaking havoc in people's lives, can we point them to an answer for their frustration and pain in the wonderful grace of Jesus that goes deeper far than all their sin and shame – believer and not-yet-believer alike?

Yes, we can.

Old Dan. He is a buzzard and he does not die easily. But God is the Master Silversmith who does not give up easily – or ever. He patiently plies his craft and over time makes me more and more like him and less and less like the person I used to be, as he burns away what is increasingly less and less of Old Dan.

That's the fuller and deeper Good News I think our people need to hear, understand, embrace, experience, live and share. They know their own "Old Dan." What they also need to know is that there is grace to overcome the domination of the "deeper down and further back" through the moment by moment, step by step, day by day surrender to the all-powerful holy love of God.

As our Christmas carol boldly proclaims, this grace reaches "far as the curse is found." Even though the stable was messy, it was also holy. Even though the stable was holy, it was also messy. So our messy lives, surrendered to God, can be a messy but holy place where God chooses to dwell supreme in power, peace and purity, to his glory.

I sincerely believe that is something this generation desires, can understand and embrace, if we will just share it with them.

CHAPTER NINE

ERADICATION

The old-timers understood sin and took it seriously. They also had high confidence in the power of God to deal with the sin problem in the human race. About sin, they used words like depravity and "inbred" sin. They used terms like carnality and the flesh to describe the arena in which sin operated. And they used radical words like eradication and crucifixion to describe the solution to the sin problem. It all went back to Adam, the original sinner.

In Adam's fall, the dynamic changed in human nature. We are now under what they termed the curse. Our relationship with God is broken and our relationships with each other are broken. We are broken, way down deep.

There were a couple of unfortunate consequences to their choice of terms. They left the accidental inference that sin was somehow a material substance to be purged out of human nature. It's not. It's dynamic and relational. And by using crucifixion language, they also left the accidental inference that sin could be dealt with once and for all by some kind of radical death to it. It can't, because it is not material, it is dynamic and relational. It operates in the flesh but it is not fleshly.

It is a power. An influence. A downward pull. A brokenness. A selfish orientation toward personal exaltation. A rebellion against God and his rightful rule. It is dealt with through breaking its power, through eroding its influence, through a stronger pull upward, through ongoing healing that leads to spiritual and relational health, through dethroning the self-centered love turned inward and placing Christ in his proper place on the throne of our lives, turning our love upward and outward.

But they were right in taking it seriously, and having the confidence that there is a solution in the love of God for us, the sacrifice of Christ for our sin, and the overcoming power of the Holy Spirit operating in every area of our lives.

It is important to note in fairness and accuracy, as well as in a spirit of appreciation, The Wesleyan Church precedent bodies, the Pilgrim Holiness Church, The Wesleyan Methodist Church and the Reformed Baptist Church of Canada, early on abandoned the "eradication" language and concepts as unrealistic and of insufficient biblical support, although many of the other American Holiness Movement Churches retained both in their preaching and in their formal theological documents.

The old-timers used crucifixion language when they talked about dealing with "original sin," specifically in the context of God's work of grace in sanctification. They used root-it-out words like eradication. They wanted that old stump of sin uprooted and hauled off. They wanted that root of bitterness pulled up and thrown away. And they could smell the suppression heresy (their opinion) of the Keswicks a mile away. This was radical. This was final. This was full and complete. This was in a word, entire.

This was also not true to the Bible or true to life.

Many scholars of the past in the Movement built major pieces of the theory on minor foundations. One of those was to claim that Paul's use of the aorist tense in the New Testament Greek in many of their favorite passages sealed the deal on the "completeness" or the "once and for all" nature of the act of "entire sanctification" (their term from Wesley). I am not a Greek scholar by any stretch of the imagination. Truth is, I did my time in Greek class and walked away a free man. But I know this. Greek scholars who have no prejudiced orientation would not support this understanding of that verb tense. Basically, the aorist tense is understood as saying something happened, and that's it. It is the context in which the verb is used, and not the tense itself, that determines the when and the how long. Rather than being an airtight tense, it is the most malleable of the tenses. And to build a cardinal piece of the doctrine on such a flimsy piece of theory is only going to lead, eventually, to the demise of that piece of the teaching at the hands of people who know better. That does not negate the truth of the reality and the depth of the work of grace we know as sanctification. It does, however, eventually force those who proclaim it, to be intellectually honest and not make claims the text does not support.

Does the grace of God reach to the untold depths of the human abyss where Old Dan (my term for my sin nature) roams in the darkness? We want to believe so, as holiness Christians. David said it reached even to the deepest hell, whatever his understanding of "sheol" was. But can it really be rooted out?

The old-timers would not agree with me on this, but here is what I think. Again, I am not a scholar or psychologist. I think God does deal with it head on, but not in the way the American Holiness Movement claimed – digging it out and throwing it away for it never to appear in us again. I think he lets Old Dan bubble to the surface, bit by embarrassing bit, in relational activity with him and with

70

others, then he drags that hurtful action or word or attitude out into the light, points at it and calls it what it is, and insists that we deal with it. Piece by piece. Event by event. Encounter by encounter. Embarrassment by embarrassment. He breaks the power of sin in our lives through his ongoing and thorough purifying process. Like the silversmith of old, he keeps the heat on us until the dross floats to the surface, is skimmed off, and his image becomes clearer and clearer in the reflection. The silver that is me becomes purer and purer. It is a process.

Since our relationship with God and those around us is dynamic and constantly changing, so our offenses and harmful actions or attitudes dynamically change those relationships as we walk together. We say something or do something that hits God or our neighbor in the wrong way. Conviction bears on our hearts. We are convinced of the need to apologize, to make amends, to make restitution, to patch things up. And this goes on forever, between us and God and everyone else we relate to. The grace to continue in this evolving dynamic relationship, and do whatever is necessary to keep it going, is sanctifying grace. It's the grace that pushes and pulls us forward in our marriage, our friendships, our relationship with acquaintances, and in our salvation.

This is not to say that we are doomed to just stumble along and repeat our struggles over and over, day after day. Just the opposite. As we are being purified by the ongoing sanctifying process, we become stronger, more consistent in our obedience, more empowered to resist temptation, more able to live in a pleasing manner for God, more prone to seek and desire his will over our own, more likely to put others first, and more driven to share the Good News with conviction and effectiveness.

This is an exciting, fulfilling life.

71

This sanctified life is not a matter of scientific formula or mechanical operation. It is dynamic and relational in nature, just as we are. My fuss with the old-timers is not that they were hypocrites who claimed things they did not possess. They were good people earnest in their pursuit of more of God in their lives. We would do well to emulate their sincerity and faith. It was the real deal. While we may think their teachings may have fallen short or missed the mark in critical places, their lives for the vast majority were right on target. They were people of their day, enamored with the Industrial Revolution and the American Dream, and they allowed themselves to be drawn into trying to describe and define a Divine Dynamic in humanistic terms and reductionist formulas. It doesn't work that way. But that does not diminish the reality of the sanctified life properly understood.

There is a cure for "Old Dan" and it is found in the overcoming power of the Holy Spirit continuously purifying us through sanctifying grace, as we grow stronger and more consistent in our obedience, and more like him in our character.

And one day, "Old Dan" will be fully and totally cleansed away, and the glorified "New Dan" will humbly bow in glory, in love, and appreciation before the Savior who saves completely.

CHAPTER TEN

TOTAL DEPRAVITY

"Total depravity" is the theological concept that, apart from God, there is absolutely nothing in us that is good. If his grace is not present in us, nothing in us is good.

Is this true, and is there a Wesleyan narrative that helps us understand the depth of our depravity and the power of God's grace?

Wesleyans have an optimistic view of grace.

In the fifth book of Psalms, there is a subset of fifteen Psalms called the Songs of Ascent. Written by David, pilgrims sang these songs as they ascended up to Jerusalem on their way to celebrate one or other of the major Jewish festivals.

My friend, Pastor Marc Johnson, made this observation about Psalm 133. As the pilgrims ascended toward the city singing how beautiful it is when God's people dwell together in unity, the Lord's blessings descended upon them. Like the dew from Mt. Herman finding its way down to Mt. Zion. Like the anointing oil poured over the head of Aaron, finding its way down his beard, over his robes and pooling at his feet.

As we move toward God, at his invitation, we find him moving toward us in mercy and grace. As we ascend toward him, we find he has already descended to where we are. As we reach out, we receive his response. As we move up, grace flows down.

Who moved first? Us to him, or him to us?

Here is where we Wesleyans offer to the rest of the church one of the most beautiful, positive and encouraging truths anyone has ever heard. And it is a cornerstone of Wesleyan theological understanding and proclamation, at the center of everything our spiritual grandfather, John Wesley, believed and preached. God moved first.

It's called prevenient grace.

It's why, I contend, that total depravity may exist on paper, and can even be found in some of Wesley's preaching, but has never existed in human experience in actuality. Why? Because from the beginning there has never been a single human being who has ever existed apart from the prevenient grace of God. Not one. Not the first. Not the worst. Not you. Not me. We have all lived in the prevenient grace of God that has faithfully and persistently sought us every moment of our lives.

That sound you just heard is the theologians jumping to their feet, their chairs turning over, ordering me out of the room and telling me never to come back. They're probably right, and I'm probably a heretic on this point.

But here's my point. Without that prevenient grace, yes, we would be totally depraved. But we have never been without that. I will surrender my point if you can name for me any person who has ever existed who was not a recipient, always, of prevenient grace.

When we were not even aware of God, he was aware of us and drew us to himself. When we were wandering lost from God, he met us face-to-face at every turn in our road and drew us to himself. When we sinned boldly, he spared us mercifully and drew us to himself. When we spat on the ground in contempt at the mention of his name, he loved us anyway and drew us to himself. When we were totally clueless about the poverty of our spiritual lives and the eternal peril that loomed over us, he covered us in his mercy and grace and continued to draw us to himself.

When we — Lord have mercy! — killed the Darling of Heaven, in his profound and incomprehensible love, he allowed that Sacrifice to be our Atonement, drawing us in mercy and grace to himself. I weep at the thought.

No matter how bad we've been. No matter how twisted we have become. No matter how far we feel we have drifted away, the trip home is always just one step. Because God is there, always drawing us to himself.

All this happened before we ever experienced saving grace. This was the grace that went before saving grace.

In the same way, once we received his grace in salvation, he continued to call us deeper in sanctification. As we drew near to him we found he had already drawn near to us. As we made sacrifices of contrition and consecration, he blessed those acts because he authored those acts in our spirits. We found that the grace of his holiness was not dependent on those acts of faith, but in fact, those acts of faith spring from his gifts of grace. Through them, he was bringing to us his sanctifying grace. And the work was his to do in us, not ours to do for him, or ours to do to try to make ourselves holy. He who calls us is faithful, and he will do it. Always, in response to our moving toward him, he will do it. God always moves first. God always moves faithfully. God always responds in transforming grace. It is who he is. It is what he does.

And that grace flows down on us like anointing oil and like the dew from heaven. We do not conjure it up. We do not make it happen. We do not work to win it by striving harder. It is the faithful, ever-flowing grace of God. We experience it when we turn our face toward him and ascend in our spirit in his direction.

This is what it looks like as a path. This is the order of salvation as Wesleyans understand it.

We were created in the Image of God

Prevenient grace was active toward us from the start

We were marred by the Fall
    We were totally lost without God
    We were totally loved by God

We were spiritually awakened by the Holy Spirit
  We experienced conviction
  We made confession
  We experienced conversion
  We made consecration
    Through the repenting of sin
    Through the receiving of Christ
    Through the role of faith
We experienced justification
We experienced regeneration
We experienced adoption
We experienced sanctification
We received the assurance of our salvation, the witness of the Spirit

We began growing in grace
We experienced sanctification through and through

We continued progressing in sanctification, growing in grace at an accelerated pace

We will continue progressing in sanctification until we die

When we die, we will experience glorification

That's a great path to be on. Anyone can understand that. And anyone should desire that. Instead of focusing on how depraved we might be, let's talk about how good God is to offer us his optimistic grace.

CHAPTER ELEVEN

ENTIRE SANCTIFICATION

Is there then such a thing as "entire sanctification?"

Yes and no. Yes as the Bible teaches it. Not so much as some of the holiness zealots taught it.

In his desire to raise the value of the sanctifying work of the Holy Spirit in the lives of believers, John Wesley used the term "entire sanctification" to describe the state of grace that results from God's full acceptance of our full surrender. It is used as a watershed term in Wesleyan theology. It delineates the phase of Christian experience that is marked by an ongoing full surrender to the will of God, a moment by moment obedience to his direction, a life at peace with God and others, with a corresponding cleansing of the heart from its selfish orientation and ambitions, and an ongoing experience of being motivated by holy love for God and others, as well as growing in grace in a way that produces maturity and increases our resemblance to the holy character of God. This is all produced by the operation of God's grace in us – initiated by him and driven by him – and is not produced by our personal striving to make ourselves holy. Love is the proof of this grace operating in our lives.

While I understand the intent of Wesley and his followers (that would be us), in my opinion, "entire sanctification" is an unfortunate phrase. I feel that way for at least three reasons.

First, the phrase "entire sanctification" does not appear in that form in the New Testament text. The Apostle Paul clearly and unapologetically proclaims that the will of God for us is our sanctification, and he describes that experience as being sanctified "through and through" by the gracious work of God in our lives. That's the term we should use. Everybody understands that.

Second, the intention to focus on this phase of the work of God in our lives is well-meaning, and frankly needed. But the unintentional consequence of this decision became an unfortunate elevation of "sanctification" above the other works of grace in our salvation process. It put the grace of justification, regeneration, adoption, and initial sanctification as a whole in the shade. Some well-meaning proclaimers of holiness would go so far as to say that if a person was not entirely sanctified (using their definitions and understanding), they were not going to heaven. Wesley never claimed that, but some of his ill-informed followers did. Of course, that claim is not true. But that was one of the unfortunate results of the elevation of this concept in holiness circles. To outsiders, it seemed we were demeaning the wonderful joy of being "saved." Saved and sanctified was our mantra!

The third unfortunate part of the use of this phrase or concept is that "entire" is so easily misunderstood. It's not entire as in, once a specific something happens in your life your religious needs are met and all the work God ever intended to do in you is complete, and you have arrived – here's your halo. People of the younger generation who do not find this claim in scripture, nor have they seen the level of perfect performance in their own life or the lives of others, find the claim of being "entirely sanctified" as arrogant and hypocritical.

Given all of that, we need to find a way to communicate this wonderful truth of a life filled with the holy love of God that this generation can understand it, believe it to be possible, and be moved to embrace it, experience it and share it with others.

Here is the corrective I would suggest.

"Entire" is entire less in terms of complete as in terms of reach, in terms of scope. It is not a claim of completion in the sense that we have fully arrived in our spiritual maturity, as though we are claiming that God has done everything in our lives he ever needs to do. "Entire" means that the sanctifying grace of God flows to every corner of our life. It reaches every nook and cranny of our life – even as far as the "deeper down and farther back" – and as we permit, it is enabled to address our faulty orientation toward ourselves and bit by bit reorient us outward toward God and our neighbor in ever-redeemed relationships.

Unless we dam it up.

When that happens, we revert to being more self-oriented and less God-oriented and others-oriented. We become focused on ourselves and the flow of his grace in our lives is hindered.

Also, this is not about personal sin management. This is about the grace of God in the form of his holy love filling us, transforming us, and overflowing into the lives of those around us. If it stops with us, it is not New Testament holiness.

I'm with Paul. "May God himself, the God of peace, sanctify you through and through. May your whole spirit, soul and body be kept blameless at the coming of our Lord Jesus Christ. The one who calls you is faithful, and he will do it." 1 Thessalonians 5:23-24 NIV

May everything that is me be open and receptive to everything that God wants to do in, with and through me, at his complete discretion as I am at his complete disposal – every part of me, through and through. Save me. Cleanse me. Fill me. Use me. All of me. Entirely.

CHAPTER TWELVE

SECOND BLESSING HOLINESS

The previous generations were insistent on talking about the "second" blessing they knew as "sanctification." For the advanced among us, the total phrasing, in this order, was: "a second definite work of grace subsequent to regeneration." This was the Wesleyan shibboleth. If you couldn't say it this way, your place in the family was highly questionable.

Here is the Wesleyan understanding updated in narrative form.

When a person is converted, there are four "blessings" that are given through the saving grace of God. Theologians call them the Concomitant Blessings, which simply means that they happen at the same time. Those blessings are justification, regeneration, sanctification and adoption. They are each both instantaneous and ongoing. They each have their starting point at the moment of conversion.

Justification is the grace of forgiveness. Our sins are not counted against us anymore. Our slate of transgressions is erased. We get a new start. This establishes our ongoing relationship with God in peace and fellowship.

Regeneration is the grace of the new birth. We are recreated into a new creation. By the power of the cross and the resurrection, we are given new life. Made new. This is our ongoing life in Christ, vibrant with resurrection power.

Sanctification is the grace of cleansing and mending and growing. The Holy Spirit begins the process in our life of washing us clean and remaking us into the Image of God. This is the initial cleaning of the house to make it fit for the King of Glory to abide there. This cleansing is ongoing, continuing as we live in obedience to the Holy Spirit.

Adoption is the grace of belonging. By the act of God's favor, we are brought into the family of God. We are the returning prodigals who are welcomed with open arms by our loving Father. This gives us our ongoing identity as a child of God.

All of these begin in us instantaneously. And all of these are designed to continue together to bring us into ever-increasing maturity as believers, as converts, as members of God's family. The rate of our growth is impacted by various realities of life, but the one we can control is perhaps the most critical in the growth process: our moment-by-moment obedience to the promptings of the Holy Spirit. Learning to say "yes" to God may well be our most vital spiritual practice of grace.

The American Holiness Movement desired to get the message of "holiness" into the church and into the world. They found it beneficial in communication to streamline their terms and simplify their vocabulary. So they spoke in terms of salvation and sanctification. This worked for their purposes because their real target was the sanctification aspect of a believer's journey with Christ.

Then they cranked it up a notch by delineating a stark contrast between the "first" work of grace, which they termed "salvation", and the "second" work of grace, which they called "sanctification". The more theologically astute among them used the term "entire sanctification" to be more precise, but the simplified "two works of grace" approach served the movement well in getting their core message across to hungry believers who just knew there had to be more to the Christian life than what they were experiencing.

An unintended consequence of this approach, however, was to make our initial experience of saving grace seem to be some sort of inferior experience to the crowning experience of sanctifying grace. Some folks were flying coach while us holiness folks were flying first class. That drew a lot of fire from the rest of the church who felt like their glorious experience of salvation was being demeaned by this teaching.

The truth is, the grace of God's work in our lives is glorious. It is wonderful. It is beyond our ability to fully comprehend, communicate or contain. And it's not a competition between "graces." It's an ongoing work of transformation that is full of grace and glory. It's not something that can be reduced to formulas, steps or stages. It rolls on, over and through manmade concepts, and spreads to every area of our being, bringing life and joy and peace and fulfillment wherever it is allowed to flow.

It saves. It sanctifies. Eventually it will glorify. And it is too glorious and great to fit neatly and compliantly into our safe and tidy categories. Real life isn't like that and neither is real grace.

I love the American Holiness Movement and I appreciate its impact in my life. I understand the motivation to exalt the crisis experience — a "second definite work of grace" they called it — as the definitive expression of the sanctifying experience. But I have been around long enough to know one expectation is not big enough to encompass the awesomeness of the work of God's grace at all times in all places in the church and the world. That living wine will not behave. It loves to bust open our old, dry wine skins.

A friend once likened this experience to diving off a diving board. Going "all in" in our relationship with God. I asked him, "Mark, I love what you are saying. But let me ask you a question. If you dive in, but I wade in, when I get out over my head to where you are, am I any less wet that you?" The important thing is not how it happens, but that it happens.

Most people will come to a point in their Christian experience where they need to make a decision about who is going to be in charge. For some this will be a dramatic "Jesus take the wheel" crisis, and for others it may be a smooth "Ah-ha moment" transition. For some it may have to happen more than once. For all, it is an issue of obedient response to God's work of sanctification going on in them. Again, the important thing is not how it happens. What is important is that it happens.

So, in no way do I mean to discount or diminish anyone's experience. God works with us and in us however he chooses, and he knows how we are made and fits our experience to our temperament and even takes account of our expectations. He's good that way. My own experience was a clear, "second blessing" event in my life, and I've never gotten over it. I've never gotten over my conversion experience either. But in no way does someone else's experience have to match mine in order to be legitimate. It just can't be reduced to a one-size-fits-all formula.

If we experience a "second blessing," it is not greater or inferior to the "first." It is simply the overwhelming, never-ending, reckless love of God expanding our capacity so we can receive more and more of his grace. And our "yes" at that crisis moment — and all crisis moments — opens our life to greater, less hindered growth in Christlikeness, and ongoing opportunities to love our neighbor with the holy love of God.

How do we best communicate this to the rising generation? Maybe, instead of talking with them about a "second blessing", or worse — choosing not to talk about it because we don't like the terminology — maybe we could just simply talk about the importance of saying "yes" to God in those opportune moments when he is moving in our lives, so the full blessing of his grace can be released with power into our lives. Encourage them to live a life of obedience in response to all the grace God wants to pour into their lives. Responding in obedience to God's work in us is in fact the path of our sanctification.

"You were taught, with regard to your former way of life, to put off your old self, which is being corrupted by its deceitful desires; to be made new in the attitude of your minds; and put on the new self, created to be like God in true righteousness and holiness." Ephesians 4:22-24 NIV

Everyone can understand and embrace that.

CHAPTER THIRTEEN

CHRISTIAN PERFECTION

"Christian perfection" is a term used by John Wesley to communicate the work of God in the grace of sanctification that can purify the motives of our hearts. It is not "sinless perfection." It acknowledges that, as broken people living in a broken world, we can have perfect intentions, but our performance seldom is that – perfect. This is probably one of the most misunderstood phrases in holiness vocabulary and desperately needs to be redefined. Wesley himself received so much criticism from outsiders that he regretted ever using the term. "There is scarce any expression in Holy Writ which has given more offense than this. The word 'perfect' is what many cannot bear. The very sound of it is an abomination to them."

So what does it mean in today's Wesleyan narrative?

Rick Sutcliffe was a major league pitcher who played mostly for the Los Angeles Dodgers and the Chicago Cubs. He was a big guy who looked to the batter like he was throwing the ball from ten feet away by the time his lanky frame extended out from the pitcher's rubber and the ball left his hand. He could, as they say, throw bee-bees.

He was good. Really good. And he had a lot of really good days on the mound. But he had his off days, too, occasionally.

On one of those off days, he gave up home runs to three straight batters. The pitching coach called time out and walked slowly out to the mound. Big Red was already fuming when he saw him coming and that just added to his anger. He said, through gritted teeth (expletives deleted), "What are you doing out here, and what could you possibly say to me right now that could make any difference?" The old pitching coach said, "Oh, I didn't really come out here to talk to you. I came out here to give the poor fireworks guy time to catch his breath!"

We all have those times where, no matter how good we are, no matter how hard we try, the perfect performance just isn't there.

The thing about performance is, we expect it consistently from everyone around us. We just don't expect it from ourselves. We understand how we can be excused for our mistakes and deserve every measure of grace from everyone else. But we too often do not extend that grace to others.

In *The Weight of* Glory, C.S. Lewis makes us face this uncomfortable reality when he points out our tendency to excuse ourselves for things we have trouble excusing in others. About this unfortunate tendency in us, he says, "To be a Christian means to forgive the inexcusable because God has forgiven the inexcusable in you."

To understand how this works in the sanctified life, it is necessary to understand the Wesleyan understanding of sin. While everything that falls short of the perfect standard that has been established by God in the person and life of Jesus Christ is sin, not all shortcomings are accountable to the person who fell short, in the Wesleyan understanding.

What is accountable to me?

Accountable sin falls into three categories. When I know not to do something bad and do it anyway, that is sin to me and I am accountable to God for that. When I know to do something good and do not do it, that is sin to me and I am accountable to God for that. When I do something that hurts someone but I had no intention of hurting them, that also becomes accountable to me and I must make amends for that when I become aware of it. And there is no statute of limitations on these things.

So instead of talking about some form of perfect performance, maybe we should talk about the integrity of our hearts. The faithfulness of our hearts. The trustworthiness of our hearts. What did we mean to do or say? What motivated us to do that or say that? And what have been the results of what we have done or said? Is the integrity, faithfulness and trustworthiness of my heart intact?

In the words of David, "Search me, O God, and know my heart; try me, and know my thoughts; and see if there be any wicked way in me, and lead me in the way everlasting." Psalm 139:23-24

According to the psalmist, God knows my heart. That's good news. That's also bad news. Good news for the person who is wanting to be open and transparent before God and is seeking God's direction and correction. Bad news for the person who wants to make excuses. Also, God knows my thoughts. Jesus put us all under conviction when he declared that lustful or murderous thoughts were as accountable as the actions they might produce. He said that because our actions are born first in the attitudes of our hearts.
This isn't going too well for us at this point.

Then the psalmist asks for a full and thorough examination. See if there is any wicked way in me. Why would he request that? Because he knows there is one path to forgiveness, one path to freedom, one path to a full relationship with God. That is the path of open and honest confession borne out of a contrite spirit that leads to repentance.

That is the way to life everlasting.

I remember hearing David Seamands preach a sermon when I was in seminary on, "Keeping short accounts with God." And I would add, with each other. This is the path of our sanctification. Not some imagined perfect performance. Our sanctification only happens through an honest acknowledgement of our failures, when they happen, followed by an honest effort at restitution, matched by an honest hunger in our hearts for a life of obedience that honors God.

In the sanctified life, the failures in our relationship with God and our neighbor do not define who we are, because sin no longer dominates our life. But denying their presence when we fail impedes our relationships with God and others.

It's not about perfect performance. But it is about a thriving relationship with God who fills us with his grace and love, transforms us into his own image, and helps us pour grace and love out on those around us. It's about the kind of integrity of heart and life that so clearly characterized a great many of those who walked this path of holiness before us, and will characterize us and our people as we leave the baggage on the side of the road, and travel the path that will bring glory to God and good to our neighbor.

We want to live this life in such a way that our friends are glad we are holiness people.

CHAPTER FOURTEEN

HEART PURITY

One of the hallmark issues of the American Holiness Movement was heart purity. According to the testimony of Peter and the early believers, in debate about the gospel being preached to the Gentiles in Caesarea, the sign the advocates pointed to regarding them being filled with the Spirit, was a pure heart. Peter declared, "God, who knows the heart, showed that he accepted them by giving the Holy Spirit to them, just as he did to us. He did not discriminate between us and them, for he purified their hearts by faith." Acts 25:8-9

But how do you know someone has a pure heart?

God knows, because unlike us he looks at the heart. But we have to rely on other indicators. Those indicators are our attitudes and our actions and our conversations.

These spring from our heart. Proverbs 4:23 says, "Above all else, guard your heart, for it is the wellspring of life." If you or someone you love served in the Marines at Camp Lejeune from the 1950s through the 1980s, you know all about the deadly impact of contaminated wellsprings. A contaminated heart poisons the entire life. A pure heart, however, produces pure actions and pure attitudes and pure speech. If you are on the receiving end of either of those heart conditions, you are aware of the toxic and the healthy. That's the sign of the condition of the heart.

Jesus, echoing Proverbs 15:7, said that what is in our heart comes out of our mouth. Good or evil. Wisdom or foolishness. If you are on the receiving end of curses or blessings, you know the difference and you know the condition of that person's heart.

That's how you know.

So, based on what we see in the Word and what we sense from the leading of the Spirit, are we thinking like we ought to think and, out of that, are we acting like we ought to act? Are we talking like we ought to talk? It really is that simple.

John Wesley understood heart purity did not stay in the heart. Again, we hear his word on purity of relationships:

> "Holy Solitaries" is a phrase no more consistent with the gospel than holy adulterers. The gospel of Christ knows of no religion, but social; no holiness but social holiness.

This is a direct echo from the words of Jesus. Love God with all you are and love your neighbor the same way you love yourself. If it does not go beyond the heart, it is not New Testament holiness. If it does not make a difference in your family's life, in your neighbor's life, in the life of the downcast and alienated, if it doesn't make a difference in your dog's life — it's not the real thing.

It is interesting for our sex-saturated culture that Wesley pointed to sexual purity here as an indisputable evidence of heart purity. Paul did the same thing.

> "For this is the will of God, your sanctification: that you should abstain from sexual immorality; that each of you

should know how to possess his own vessel in sanctification and honor, not in passion of lust, like the Gentiles who do not know God; that no one should take advantage of and defraud his brother in this matter, because the Lord is the avenger of all such, as we also forewarned you and testified. For God did not call us to uncleanness, but in holiness. Therefore, he who rejects this does not reject man, but God, who has also given us His Holy Spirit."

1 Thessalonians 4:3-8 NKJV

Our rising generation may not understand the terminology of heart purity, but they understand the need of it. They understand the need to be a better person from the inside out.

We must all take caution, however, to help them understand it's not about just trying to be a better person in their own effort. That is an easy snare into which to fall for our self-help, pride-saturated culture. It is the heart-purifying work of the Holy Spirit that makes us a better person. It's not thinking better and doing better and talking better that makes us better. It's being made better by the sanctifying grace of the Holy Spirit that results in holy love expressed in our thoughts, our words, our actions, springing from a cleansed and guarded heart.

Since, as Paul says, "This is the will of God, your sanctification," that carries with it not only the will of God but the promise of God. "The one who called you is faithful, and he will do it."

While "heart purity" may not translate well to our younger friends, being made better from the inside out certainly will.

Here is our prayer from our Grandfather Wesley's Mother Church, the Church of England, known as a Collect for Purity of Heart:

Almighty God, unto whom all hearts are open, all desires known, and from whom no secrets are hid: Cleanse the thoughts of our hearts by the inspiration of your Holy Spirit, we pray, that we may perfectly love you, and worthily magnify your holy Name; through Christ our Lord. Amen.

Here is our prayer from scripture, asking for a pure and steadfast heart – a heart of integrity, faithfulness and trustworthiness:

Create in me a pure heart, O God,
and renew a steadfast spirit within me.
Do not cast me from your presence
or take your Holy Spirit from me.
Restore to me the joy of your salvation
and grant me a willing spirit, to sustain me.
Then I will teach transgressors your ways,
so that sinners will turn back to you.

Psalm 51:10-13 NIV

CHAPTER FIFTEEN

BITTERNESS AND RESENTMENT

A pure heart is one thing. A polluted heart is something else altogether.

Among the more common, toxic pollutants of the human heart is the spirit of jealousy, which manifests itself, among other ways, in bitterness and resentment. These negative dynamics emerge in a person's heart when hurt happens. The old holiness preachers were consistent in warning their people to guard against allowing a root of bitterness to become imbedded in their hearts through hurt or harm.

My friend, Dan Croy, used to share a session in his marriage retreats on where hurt and anger takes us in our relationships with each other. This is my take on the ideas I remember Dan sharing.

Hurt produces anger, which is a natural human emotion, and an understandable response to hurt in all its dimensions – including personal slight, physical harm, acts of injustice, perceived unfairness, being slighted or discriminated against, cheated, cheated on, lied about, publically embarrassed, and so on. The list is endless, really.

The hurt puts us on a path of response that brings us face-to-face with a yield sign. Will we yield to the impulse of the flesh, or will we yield to the impression of the Spirit?

When we yield to the impulse of the flesh, we walk a path that leads us to bitterness and resentment, which may lead to some of the more heated passions – hatred, rage, or even verbal or physical attack. Or it may lead to the more passive-aggressive responses, which are no less corrosive and no less harmful. These tend to sit there and rot our spirits, leaking out on others when they jostle us. Not pretty.

The path of fleshly (selfish) response leads to unforgiveness and broken relationships.

But if we yield to the impression of the Spirit, we travel a path of contrition, a broken heart, a spirit of remorse, which leads to repentance, confession, apology, reconciliation, and a restored relationship. The scars may not go away, but they will be transformed into witnesses of the goodness of God and the power of forgiveness. That's beautiful.

For the person being sanctified, a quick and consistent yielding to the impression of the Spirit, and a resistance to the impulse of the flesh, is the desired response in times of temptation, including the temptation to harbor anger. But occasionally that person may wander down the wrong path. But we do not walk that path alone. The Holy Spirit is faithful to walk that path with us. And he will nudge us to turn around. He will place a heaviness of conviction on our hearts. He won't even let us enjoy our self-proclaimed justified anger. He will hold up a mirror to our face to show us the clouded countenance that gives away our clouded heart. He will make us uncomfortable. He will make us miserable. He will take away our joy. He will make the brook dry up on us to make sure we don't hang around where we're not supposed to be. Things that should taste like honey in our mouth now taste like sand. And he is not hesitant – like your mama – to get in your face and tell you to straighten up.

That is his job.

When we turn in repentance and begin to walk the path of reconciliation and restoration, the weight lifts, the joy returns, times of refreshing return to our hearts, and we again experience the smile of God's approval on our life.

The old holiness folks knew the reality of this life, and they knew the wisdom of walking with God and their fellow Pilgrims on the path of holiness, as well as the peril of walking away from God and their family and friends. Again, they knew the truth of Proverbs 4:23 . . .

> "Above all else, guard your heart, for it is the wellspring of life."

And so they knew the wisdom of living a careful, Spirit-directed life. In doing so, they were not only better (not bitter) people, but by living in obedient response to the Spirit, they put themselves in a position to be used of God to reach the lost, bless their neighbors, save the world and move the kingdom forward. That's a great place to be.

> "Get rid of all bitterness, rage and anger, brawling and slander, along with every form of malice. Be kind and compassionate to one another, forgiving each other, just as in Christ God forgave you."
>
> Ephesians 4:31-32 NIV

97

CHAPTER SIXTEEN

TOTAL CONSECRATION

This generation of Wesleyans, following the Baptists as we are prone to do, understands the human side of the sanctification process — consecration, dedication, being fully devoted followers of Christ — and accepts it as valid and reasonable. What they do not seem to grasp is God's side of the equation — sanctifying grace flowing throughout their entire being and flowing from them into every area where they have influence.

Like the later generations of American Holiness Movement church folks who reduced sanctification to "a pure heart" and made it all about themselves, this generation is tempted to make their level of commitment all about themselves, striving (one of their favorite words) to be holy.

Their striving is sincere and full of effort. But sanctification, as an act of God's grace working in their lives, is not about human effort. It's not about striving. It's about surrender.

My friend Tim Kirkpatrick and I have had an ongoing conversation about this generation and their understanding of holiness. One of the points he raises is that this generation totally gets the concept of being "all in." In fact, our guess is that when we ask them to share their sanctification stories, the stories will be about when they decided to walk away from their frustrating life of half-hearted service to the Lord and decided to go "all in." We also guess that for most of them, that moment will coincide with their sense of calling. At one point in our conversation, Tim sent me a picture of something he had used as an illustration of this concept in one of his speaking engagements for The Wesleyan Church in Australia. It was a poker chip!

After my initial response of "Dude, you can't use a poker chip as an illustration among Wesleyans," I calmed down and admitted that though John Wesley would likely cringe at the thought, Charles would get a kick out of it, seeing he borrowed all those popular bar tunes in his day for melodies for his hymns and gospel songs!

So let me ask you this.

Can you point to a time or place in the writings of John Wesley where he definitively declares a claim to entire sanctification?

He preached it. He taught it. He expected it of his preachers and people. He and his brother wrote a ton of songs about it. He even declared it to be the "Grand Depositum" of the Methodist movement.

Yet the great recoverer of the doctrine of holy love filling the heart and expelling sin that came down to us from Jesus and John and Paul never was so bold as to declare his personal experience of entire sanctification.

But if we asked the question differently, what would we say?

That question: What was John Wesley's "all in" moment?

To a person, we would all answer with one word, "Aldersgate!"

"In the evening I went very unwillingly to a society in Aldersgate Street, where one was reading Luther's 'Preface to the Epistle to the Romans'. About a quarter before nine, while he was describing the change which God works in the heart through faith in Christ, I felt my heart strangely warmed. I felt I did trust in Christ, Christ alone for salvation, and an assurance was given me that he had taken away my sins, even mine, and saved me from the law of sin and death."

There is no doubt that a conversion took place that evening. Wesley himself would liken it to no less than his moving in relationship to God from "a slave" to "a son."

It formed in him his sense of the assurance of salvation, and consequently the development of that assurance as a cornerstone doctrine in his theological understanding, and arguably the most impactful contribution he has made across the board in Christian theology.

But in addition, the Aldersgate encounter also marks what appears to be his abandoning of his works-oriented religion in favor of receiving the grace of God that brought him into a brand new depth of relationship with the Lord. It was a moment of total surrender of everything in which he had placed his trust, and the full embrace of everything God had to offer in its place. Full surrender. Total trust. Absolute sacrifice. And an assurance that his surrender, trust and sacrifice was fully accepted and accompanied with a cleansing of his heart — "he had taken away my sins, even mine, and saved me from the law of sin and death."

That is a beautiful testimony of conversion. But it is more. It is a clear echo from John. "If we confess our sins, he is faithful and just,

100

and will forgive our sins, and cleanse us from all unrighteousness."
Wesley himself gave this testimony of his Aldersgate experience in a
letter to his older brother Samuel, written on October 30, 1738: "By
a Christian, I mean one who so believes in Christ, as that sin hath no
more dominion over him; and in this obvious sense of the word I
was not a Christian till May 24th last past. For till then sin hath the
dominion over me, although I fought with it continually; but surely,
then, from that time to this it hath not; — such is the free grace of
God in Christ."

My point is that Wesley uses a description here of God's grace
overcoming the domination of sin in his life that he normally later
uses to describe the experience of entire sanctification. I am not so
presumptuous as to instruct Mr. Wesley regarding his experience
with God, but from our perspective nearly 300 years later, it sure
looks like it from here.

Our friend and holiness advocate Keith Drury gave this beautiful
description of the sanctifying grace of God in his *Holiness for
Ordinary People*:

> God through His Holy Spirit will rush into the very center of
> your life. He will fill you with His Spirit. He will perform a
> major spiritual miracle. When you were saved you received
> all of the Holy Spirit. But now the Holy Spirit gets all of
> you.... The Holy Spirit will now move into all areas of your
> fully consecrated life. You can consecrate all to God. God
> will then sanctify all of you in response. Once you have
> surrendered your all to God, He is now unhindered by your
> internal resistance. Now God is free to perform a radical,
> internal cleansing and unleashing of spiritual power.

That is going "all in."

CHAPTER SEVENTEEN

AVOIDING THE APPEARANCE OF EVIL

One of the lenses through which our behavior as sanctified Christians was viewed back in the day was, "avoiding the very appearance of evil," with major emphasis on appearance.

When I was in college at Southern Pilgrim in Kernersville, we had a very clear and direct understanding about what we could do and couldn't do, what we could wear and what we couldn't wear, what we could say and couldn't say, where we could go and not go.

One of the places we couldn't go was Spiro's Café in downtown Kernersville. Spiro sold beer.

Spiro was Greek. Johnny Wheeler, one of our ministerial students who was married and lived off campus, would go in there on a regular basis, take a seat in a back booth, and work on school work. Holiness school work. In the process, he would engage Spiro in conversations about what he was learning in Mrs. Gardner's New Testament greek class. They became friends, and the conversation went way beyond ancient and modern languages. He did find out there is a lot of difference, apparently, between *koine* greek and modern greek. I don't recall Mrs. Gardner being particularly enamored with Johnny's modern greek observations in her New Testament greek class. She might have been scandalized if she knew where he was getting his information.

Spiro, as you might guess, sold the best pizza in town. I can't tell you how I know that, but I can tell you that I definitely know that. So who was the greater sinner here? Johnny, the holiness ministerial student who walked boldly into Spiro's Café, past the bar and the beer, and engaged this icon of Kernersville in conversations about greek and Jesus, against the rules? Or this other guy we know who sneaked in there from time to time, and never engaged Spiro in conversation, but grabbed his pizza and ran, because Spiro sold beer, therefore pizza from Spiro's was against the rules?

I think you know.

CHAPTER EIGHTEEN

WORDLINESS

One of the most common concerns of our holiness ancestors was "worldliness." This was a defining factor in "holiness" understanding, and so was often the subject of much of our preaching. If you wanted to be accepted by this crowd, you did not want to be labeled worldly.

Worldliness in the distant Wesleyan past was understood and defined in terms of how a person looked, how a person dressed, how a person interacted with others (especially of the opposite gender), what a person avoided in terms of addictive substances, and where a person went or would not go. What they would say, and what they would not say. What they would do and what they would not do.

We are in the world. We are not of the world. How do we work that out in our daily living of the sanctified life?

We moved from the Kentucky District to the Ohio District of the Pilgrim Holiness Church at the beginning of my junior year of high school in 1965. Merger was just around the corner.

The Ohio District was considered to be more "liberal" than the Kentucky District. This is all relative, of course. "Liberal" in this setting was synonymous with "worldly." Not liberal in theology. Nothing close to that. But they did wear short sleeves, and we suspected they had televisions hidden away somewhere in their houses.

104

My first visit to the Conference Camp Grounds in Coshocton that next summer confirmed all suspicions. To my shock, there was a pastor who drove a brand-new Buick Riviera. I had been scandalized in Kentucky when one of the pastors drove onto the campground in a sporty new Corvair. That was too much. But this guy in Ohio is driving a Riviera! A Riviera was as close as a Wesleyan preacher could get to driving a Cadillac. It was almost more than my developing little Pharisee self could take. And besides that, he was loud and flashy. He wore cuff links. He was, in a word, worldly.

At the same time, one of the leading churches in the district, which happened to be across town from us, had made a big ruckus about the merger and pulled out of the denomination. This was a very conservative church. Unlike the worldly pastor, the pastor of this church not only would not be boisterous or flashy — he refused to wear a necktie with his dark suit, because a necktie was too worldly for him.

Dad and I visited that church during one of their revival meetings. The lasting memory for me of that evening was seeing a picture of Billy Graham taped to a post in the sanctuary. Hand-written on the picture were the words, "Hill Billy Graham Cracker." I think he was wearing swimming trunks in the picture. Maybe that was the problem.

On our Pilgrim college campus, girls in short skirts —this was the day of the mini-skirt — were subject to be brought into the office of the Dean of Women to have their hems measured to see if they were within the parameters of the established "at the knee" limits.

That day certainly had its strange things it was willing to fight about and break fellowship over.

Grabbing hold of a consensus on what was worldly and what was not always seemed to be quite a challenge for mid-century holiness people. To borrow a famous statement from the courts regarding another hold-the-line kind of issue, the holiness folk adopted a very subjective, sometimes tribe specific, attitude about worldliness,

105

described as, "I may not be able to define it, but I know it when I see it."

For my generation and younger, we all walked away from that.

For anyone in this current culture desiring to live in a way that is in the world but not of the world, the more proper understanding of "worldliness" is in spirit and attitude more than in appearance, although modesty in appearance counts more than some want to admit.

It is a matter of choices, some in secret. What do you watch on television and cable? How do you conduct yourself in isolation on social media? For the first time, our access to pornographic material is free and constantly available. Everyone ahead of us had to go through someone else to get it. We carry it in our pocket on our smart phone.

So, it's not so much about how you look. It's about how you look at things.

The previous generation was concerned about such things as modesty (which included no pants or shorts for women, and no one was to go "mixed bathing," their term for swimming), a prideful look (which included no wearing of make-up, no short or dyed hair, and no wearing jewelry for women, and toned down clothing for men, no shorts, and no long hair), sobriety (which meant total abstinence from beverage alcohol, no tobacco, and no use of addictive substances, or working in stores that sold these things), virtue (which meant chaste relationships between the genders), and vanity (which was the catch-all category for whatever vices they might have missed). This of course is far from an exhaustive list.

This was the worldliness that was to be avoided by God's people and not brought into God's church. This was the original 4H Club: "hair, hems, hose and hellevision."

You will notice these are all issues that are expressed outwardly.

106

The rising generation has its list of concerns as well. They include systemic evil and racism, consumerism, gender issues and attractions, austerity, global environmental issues, authenticity, equality, inclusiveness, justice, plurality, and the rights of any person or group who might be disenfranchised or discriminated against. Whether the older generation likes it or not, these are actually Christian values that have been co-opted and redefined by the Post-Christian culture, many times outside a Christian morality orientation.

You will notice these are also outward-oriented issues that express themselves from the heart.

I think the next generation has Jesus on their side. He dealt with folks who took careful living to an extreme. His piercing criticism was, "You give a tenth of your spices—mint, dill and cumin. But you have neglected the more important matters of the law—justice, mercy and faithfulness. You should have practiced the latter, without neglecting the former." Matthew 23:23 NIV

Both lists of issues have merit and should be given serious consideration in the sanctified life. The key is balance, and understanding that some things are weightier than others. Our inner and outer expressions of living a life of holy love should always be marked by the full embrace of justice, mercy and faithfulness. That is from the mouth of Jesus himself. Or, as the old Pilgrim Holiness motto used to say (borrowed from the French Revolution, sanctified, and redeemed),

"In essentials, unity.
In non-essentials, liberty.
In all things, charity."

Will we survive in this challenging culture so dominated by the spirit of the world? Of course we will, if we're made of the same stuff the early church was. They were able to shine like stars in the darkness of First Century culture, and ours is increasingly similar. It's a matter of small, daily, moment-by-moment choices which – over time and directed by the Holy Spirit – become a consistent, convincing life in a culture of darkness and death.

CHAPTER NINETEEN

PUTTING OFF THE OLD MAN
PUTTING ON THE NEW MAN

There is this "exchanged life" that takes place in the process of our sanctification. Putting off what scripture calls "the old man" (or person) and putting on what scripture calls "the new man" (or person). You can find biblical expressions of and theological explanations for that concept, but this is what it looks like in narrative form.

In one of his radio broadcasts on *Insights for Living*, Evangelical Free pastor Chuck Swindoll made this observation about spiritual growth: "If we are going to go forward, we must leave Egypt behind."

He told the story (not a real story, he was just preaching) of a mom who came into the living room and saw her five children on the brand new carpet playing with some black and white furry things. They had found a family of skunks! Alarmed, she yelled, "Run, children! Run!"

And they each grabbed a skunk and ran.

It is no surprise to anyone who has any life experience at all, that there come times when a person has to make a choice to stay where they are, or to sacrifice something in order to move forward. Sometimes that's giving up a bad thing in order to do a good thing. Sometimes that's giving up a good thing to do a better thing.

Sometimes that's giving up something precious that you likely never will recover in order to give something to someone else that likely has no way to get that themselves, or pay you back.

The choice to go forward comes to us in any number of ways.

One is, limiting your options in order to capitalize on greater opportunities. Athletes understand this. People in love with each other understand this. Parents definitely understand this. And anyone on the path of sanctification will come to understand it, if they don't already.

Our early holiness ancestors certainly understood it. And they built lists of what they felt they should stop doing and lists of what they should start doing or keep doing. To no one's surprise, the "stop doing" list quickly outgrew the "keep doing" list.

Interestingly, an examination of those lists shows the "stop doing" list tended to be what they would call sins of the flesh. The other list tended to be more spiritual in nature. When you compare that to what Jesus had to say, he was a lot tougher on the spiritual sins than the fleshly ones. He didn't endorse fleshly sins, but he knew where those came from — spiritual sinfulness. He aimed at the root, not so much the fruit.

I have come into possession of a copy of the 1914-1915 *Manual of the International Apostolic Holiness Church,* a forerunner of the Pilgrim Holiness Church. This group was founded by Martin Wells Knapp in Cincinnati in 1897, loosely related to God's Bible School. The *Manual* came from the library of my hero and mentor, James C. Smith. It belonged to his mother, Carrie Estelle Smith.

James was a really good preacher, an excellent pastor, a dedicated theological educator and a dear friend. He was also the son-in-law of General Superintendent Walter L. Surbrook. To top it off, James was a proud product of our Bagley Swamp church.

In reading the *Manual*, I came away with two distinct impressions. First, these folks valued organization to a point, but they did not let

109

organization get in the way of their mission. Second, it seems they wanted to get some basic things on paper as a touch-point for their work together, but they were fluid and flexible in their methods.

Not so much with their list of expected behaviors, however.

They were specific about what they were against. Members were specifically instructed, "to avoid all places of worldly amusement … such as dances, shows, theaters, horse-races, baseball games and places where gambling is indulged in …." (paragraph 100). Paragraph 101 instructs women about their apparel and appearance, quoting verbatim 1 Timothy 2:9-11 and 1 Peter 3:3-4 (KJV), interestingly without commentary.

To their credit, these two paragraphs are preceded by paragraph 99, which addresses "putting off the old man" with his spiritual transgressions, and "putting on the new man" described as being "kind, tenderhearted, forgiving, honest, diligent and trustworthy."

Unfortunately, where this got lived out on the ground, in the local churches, it is always easier to assess the sins of the flesh than to measure the virtues of the spirit. In this atmosphere, too many times, the critical spirit was allowed to thrive and the tender, compassionate spirit got pushed aside. Taking seriously their commitment to live a careful, holy life led some to fall into the trap of strictness and severity of spirit. That led too often to a judgmental spirit, which allowed some to assume the role of sanctification sheriff. No one died and made anyone else the sanctification sheriff.

What should have been the positive, optimistic message of holiness became a dreary behavior-based religion for too many in our tribe. Their unhappiness with the spiritual tone of their own life led to a spirit of resentment toward those who were not so bound. They were named compromisers. They were confronted for not following the strict path others laid out for them. They were criticized for their joy in the Lord by people who had stifled theirs.
Some folks just weren't happy unless they were unhappy.

110

So, too many of them became known more for their sour spirit than for their contagious joy. They became known more for their long sleeves, long dresses, long pants and long faces than for the light of God shining from their countenance. They became known more for what they were against than what they were for. (I was tempted to say they identified more with the combative spirit of Paul where they found it in scripture, and too often pushed aside the tender, compassionate spirit of Jesus . . . but I'm glad I didn't say that.)

In the spirit of optimistic grace, these are the kinds of mistakes we do not want to repeat.

CHAPTER TWENTY

CONVICTIONS

People of strong conviction live by the principles which they have become convinced are trustworthy, true and, for Christians, biblical. These were people of strong convictions.

Convictions are supposed to serve as accurate expressions of the lifestyle expectations that are found in the scriptures. By nature, they are debatable, somewhat esoteric, and not universal. In the American Holiness Movement, the different "tribes" such as the Pilgrim Holiness Church, the Wesleyan Methodist Church, the Church of the Nazarene, the Churches of Christ in Christian Union, the Church of God–Anderson, the Church of God–Holiness, the Evangelical Methodist Church, the Salvation Army, the Free Methodist Church, the various individual Methodist churches that still held to holiness sympathies (most of which had some relationship with Asbury College and Seminary) and other holiness groups held to many of the same convictions, which served as a core of values held across the board. But there were also variations to each list, things held only by particular tribes, and changes across the years that were adopted by some but not by all.

These convictions, now, are what define the various camps of what is left of the American Holiness Movement. There is some residual core of those values left in the Methodists who are in the process of disaffiliating from the United Methodist Church, but that is less about holiness and more about basic biblical beliefs. The Asbury influence is the source of most of the holiness remnant that remains in the Methodist Church. On the other end of the spectrum is the conservative element of those who hold holiness convictions. They separate themselves from the rest of the movement by their strong convictions centered on behavior and appearance as their expression of their holiness beliefs. Holding the line, as they define it, is central to their fellowship. They have done a great job of bonding together, holding regional rallies and a large annual convention very well attended. God's Bible School, Hobe Sound College, and a score of other holiness schools provide training for ministers and encouragement for those committed to the cause. By and large, while there are disagreements about the current list of convictions, there remains a friendly, collegial spirit between those on the more conservative side and those more in the middle. The middle group – the Wesleyans, the Nazarenes, and the Free Methodists, among others – have moderated on the list of convictions. But their greatest moderation has been their drift away from being declarative as holiness churches, and drifting into being evangelical churches, instead.

How important are convictions? To the old-timers, they were central to their identity, both individually and as a church. And their non-universal nature became a continuous source of friction in the larger fellowship. Especially where there was disagreement or a raucous minority who wanted to impose their convictions on everyone else.

I came home from Camp Meeting one summer with the new conviction that I should be wearing long sleeves if I really was going to be a holiness young man. I was about 14, and that's what my older friend Butch Sparks told me and my friend Jimmy Clark. So long sleeves it was. Mom and Dad noticed it immediately, and Dad came up to my room to have a gentle conversation. As I recall, it went something like this: "Son, if you want to have this conviction, it is fine with your Mom and me, as long as it is from your heart, and from the Bible, and from the Lord. If it's just something someone else told you, though, you don't have to do that." I don't remember how long Jimmy held out but, as I also recall, it was in the high 90s that week, we had no air conditioning in the Pleasureville parsonage, and I was back in short sleeves by that afternoon. Wise man, my dad.

These imposed "personal convictions" worked a hardship in the Bagley Swamp Pilgrim Holiness Church against James Smith's young cousin Josiah back in the day. James was never particularly athletic. Josiah was. He loved baseball. And he was good at it. As a youngster, he wanted to play, but his church had a rule against it. And a small group of severe enforcers let him know that was not going to be acceptable.

He played anyway. Not in a spirit of defiance, but the boy just wanted to play baseball.

Those rules, of course, changed over time. When I became his pastor he was a grown man by then and a well-established farmer in the community. Everyone in Perquimans County knew Josiah Smith. He was friendly. He was funny. He was fun to be with. Full of joy, with a little harmless foolishness and a lot of mischief mixed in. But mostly they knew him as a godly man. If Josiah said it, you could take it to the bank.

Very few would have guessed he was not an official member of the Bagley Swamp Wesleyan Church. It was his church. He was one of the top three or four givers in the church, I would guess. I know he tithed the income from his chicken houses, because that money was added directly at Josiah's request to the base salary the church established for the pastor. Every twelve weeks, my salary changed, according to the amount of money the Perdue Farm Fresh Chicken Company was willing to pay Josiah for his flock. I became a stalwart prayer warrior for the health and growth of Josiah Smith's chickens!

He was true to his church in every way, but because of that old rule, he never felt like he should step across the line drawn in the sand by the old-timers way back there. Somehow I find more integrity and tender respect in his deference to them than I find in the demands they made of him. Josiah was a good, sanctified Wesleyan — member or not.

Living a careful life was taken seriously by all, but defined narrowly by too many. Their motivation is understandable. Their execution, too often, lacked grace.

From my personal perspective, I am in the generation directly following the generation that walked away from The Wesleyan Church and the other holiness churches. They just couldn't take it anymore. So they walked.

Sadly, too many of the old-timers valued their convictions more than they valued their children.

Let us commit to each other that, while biblical convictions have been created to establish virtue and value in our lives, they are not more important than people for whom Christ died. Especially our children. There is a way to live a careful, Christlike life that honors our biblical convictions while at the same time it values the people God loves so much that he gave his only Son for their redemption.

Let's find that way and walk in it.

CHAPTER TWENTY-ONE

THE CAREFUL LIFE

As a pastor, I was given a gift from the people of Bagley Swamp, a community in northeastern North Carolina, not far removed from the Great Dismal Swamp, within about an hour from the northern Outer Banks, and close enough to the Norfolk, Chesapeake, and Virginia Beach cities of tidewater Virginia that many drove there for employment (especially at the huge U.S. Naval Base there) and for major shopping.

The Bagley Swamp community, basically a group of houses on a meandering country road, predated the Revolutionary War. It was known colloquially as Smith Town, because of the three separate sets of Smiths that made up much of the small population. It was a small community in the smallest populated county in the state. Corn, soybeans and peanuts ruled the farming economy, and those farmers taught me great things about faith, as they put practically everything they owned in the ground every year and trusted God for the harvest.

"Preacher, if we got a rain right now, it would be a million dollar rain! Pray for rain!"

"Preacher, it's raining too much. We can't get into the fields, they're too wet! Pray for the rain to quit and the sun to come out."

I finally had to tell them, "Look guys, I'm in sales. I'm not in management!"

Bagley Swamp is also one of the fewest locations on the east coast where you can find rattlesnakes, copperheads and water moccasins sharing the habitat. But that's another story for another day.

The Bagley Swamp church had a long, rich history. They were a strong, holiness church. Starting out as a Methodist preaching point under Jim Smith (no relation to James or Josiah), they joined the International Apostolic Holiness Union and Prayer League (later Church) and then became a Pilgrim Holiness Church when that group formed in 1923. They had bona fide holiness credentials all the way back to their beginning. They were one of the earliest International Apostolic Holiness churches in the state, becoming one of the charter churches of what is now the North Carolina East District of The Wesleyan Church.

We know our general Wesleyan Church history. We are the product of two streams of the American Holiness Movement, the Wesleyan Methodist Church and the Pilgrim Holiness Church, flowing together in 1968 to create The Wesleyan Church.

The Wesleyan Methodists were Methodist through and through, even with their break-away history in protest against the Methodist Episcopal Church-South and the compromise of the Methodist Episcopal Church northern branch over the institution of human slavery. They brought their Methodist DNA with them into the merger with the Pilgrim Holiness Church. They were direct spiritual descendants of John Wesley.

The Pilgrims, on the other hand, were direct descendants of the American Holiness Movement, a Methodist movement which became a generation removed in relation to Wesley with their unceremonious expulsion from the Methodist Episcopal Church in 1896. Pilgrims were a broad amalgamation of like-minded holiness believers who were more like Wesley's grandchildren in their spiritual lineage.

One of the major non-Wesleyan influences in the Pilgrim Holiness group came from the large number of Quakers who heard the holiness message, embraced it, and joined the Movement. They, of course, brought with them their quiet, pietistic DNA.

Seth Cook Rees was one of the two founders of the International Apostolic Holiness Church and Prayer League (which later took the more palatable name Pilgrim Holiness Church from Rees' Pasadena congregation). His fellow founder was a Methodist, Martin Wells Knapp, who was a "come outer" who also founded God's Bible School in Cincinnati.

Although isolated in rural northeastern North Carolina, it was amazing to me to experience this same Methodist/Holiness/Quaker mixture in the Bagley Swamp church. They had an interesting mix of church backgrounds making up their history.

One of the best gifts Bagley Swamp gave to me came in the form of the Quakers who were part of the congregation. The Bagley Swamp boys tended to marry Up River Friends girls. Into the hot holiness atmosphere, the Quakers brought a tenderness and compassion that melded with the holiness fire. It was a beautiful thing to see. When the Spirit would move in the worship service — and it was rare that didn't happen — the holiness folk would rejoice while the Quakers sat with tears of joy streaming down their cheeks. It was precious.

Whoever experiences that is drawn to it.

And who wouldn't want that? Instead of a stodgy old list, it is so much better and more fulfilling to be defined as a person living the sanctified life, filled with the tender, compassionate love of Jesus. It is precisely what our world, and our people hunger for. Leaving the other behind, this is what was real from our past that we need to bring back to our future.

"Live such good lives among the pagans that, though they accuse you of doing wrong, they may see your good deeds and glorify God on the day he visits us." 1 Peter 2:12 NIV

CHAPTER TWENTY-TWO

THE VICTORY

The older generation often talked about "having the victory" as a description of their expectation of living an overcoming life. Is there a way to share this concept to today's culture that aligns with the Wesleyan narrative?

In messing with my grandchildren, I will sometimes say, "Ellis, have you still got the victory?" Ellis' response, of course, is to give me that puzzled look we have all given our grandpas when they mess with us, and he usually just walks away. Sometimes I detect a not so subtle shaking of his head, like "what language is that man speaking?"

But it plants a seed. Way down the path, Ellis might just ponder on the meaning of "victory" in his life, especially at a time when he needs it, or he might ask his cousin Owen, "Do you remember when Pappaw used to ask us if we had the victory? What do you think he meant by that?" Imagine, a theological discussion among the next generation of LeRoy boys!

Here's the deal. That question becomes intriguing to the emerging generations precisely because they haven't a clue what it means. As a provocative tool, it works. As far as clear and compelling communication goes, not so much.

Instead of talking about having "the victory" why don't we talk about being given the ability not to be dominated by sinning?

I am distinguishing here the classic Wesleyan understanding of the nature of sin: the state of sin into which we are born through no fault of our own, and the actions of sin that spring forth from that state which we have control over — doing things we should not do or not doing things we should do. The willful violation of a clear expectation.

For instance, if we mess up on a math test, that miscalculation falls short of the standard of perfection and falls into that category of "sin" described as "sinning in word, thought and deed daily." Anything less than perfect goes into that category — every time we fall short of the perfect standard whether we do that on purpose or not. But if I mess up on a math test, that is not accountable to me as deliberate sin. It is simply a mistake. However, if I cheat on that math test, that is accountable sin.

Wesleyans believe you don't have to cheat on math tests. You can choose not to cheat on math tests. That choice can be made consistently, every time the temptation is there to cheat, and in fact our lives can be characterized as people who do not habitually cheat on math tests.

We can have "the victory" over cheating on math tests. And in every other temptation offered to us, we can choose not to sin.

Will we be perfect in our behavior? No. For one thing, our tempter is smarter and more experienced than we are. He is uncanny in his ability to trip us up. But we are not alone in this daily walk. Residing within us is the Holy Spirit who guides us, guards us, warns us, shields us, protects us and enables us to say "yes" to him and "no" to temptation. Moment by moment. Decision by decision.

It's not about being perfect in our performance. It's about understanding that we no longer need to be dominated by sin or characterized by sinning. It is the ongoing, active, powerful sanctifying grace of God through the Holy Spirit that breaks the domination of sin in our lives. And by that, we continue to become less like our old sinner selves and more like him in characteristic love and holiness.

The concept of "the victory" may not communicate well with the rising generations, but this will:

"In all these things, we are more than conquerors through him who loved us." Romans 8:37

Granted, some are delivered while others must cope. In his own life, Paul experienced both. Bitten by a poisonous snake, his life was spared by miraculous, immediate healing. Yet when praying repeatedly for deliverance from his "thorn in the flesh" (whatever it may have been), he was not delivered immediately but instead was given grace to endure. He had to learn to cope. There seems to be no connection between whether you are delivered or given grace to cope and your spiritual maturity or your advanced relationship with God — sanctification. It seems there is only God's will, God's grace in whatever form he desires to give it, and God's glory — through us in all our circumstances.

But one thing is clear. There is victory. There is no need for us to be dominated by the power of sin. In Christ, and with Christ in us, we are overcomers, not overcome. Victors, not victims.

So Ellis, do you still have the victory?

CHAPTER TWENTY-THREE

IN A STATE OF GRACE

One of the phrases used in testimony among the holiness folk was to say that they were "in a state of grace." By that they meant they had moved from the entry level condition of grace marked by justification, regeneration, adoption and initial sanctification, and were now in a higher stage, a state of entire sanctification. Rather than understanding sanctification in a relational and dynamic way, they saw themselves as being measured on their position, as though they were on a line that began with being in a state of "lost," then moving to a state of "saved," then moving to a state of "sanctified," where they remained until their demise, at which time they would move to a state of being "glorified," the final destination of the sanctified believer.

Is there a better, more dynamic, way to understand our standing in grace?

Perhaps we should think and talk less in static terms and more in dynamic terms when we are talking about our spiritual growth. We need to think less in terms of stages and more in terms of dynamic upward movement.

Our spiritual life should be like the stock market in a healthy economy. There will be peaks and there may be plunges, but across the long view there should be a dynamic, detectable, even measurable growth upward. I like to refer to this pattern as the work of the Holy Spirit in us making us more and more like Christ and less and less like the person we used to be.

122

Instead of seeing ourselves in categories of spiritual maturity, perhaps we should see ourselves on a continuum that is moving upward and onward, not so much like an arrow flying straight and true, but more like an eagle who, though in a storm or strong wind, finds a way to dip and swoop and rise as he rides the currents higher.

No one in this life is going to enjoy a smooth ride. But anyone, by the grace of God filling them with holy love and enabling them to make the good, better and best choices, can find themselves being closer to God and more like him in character than they were last year.

This is one of the realities from our past that we should not lose.

CHAPTER TWENTY-FOUR

HUMILITY

One of the pitfalls of a holiness mindset is that it can tend to breed a prideful spirit in people. What an irony. Proud to be so humble. Proud to be so holy. Proud to be more humble and holy than you or your group, obviously.

The root sin in us all is pride. The spirit of Christ is a spirit of humility. As my old District Superintendent Raymond S. Shelton used to say, "Holiness and humility are twins." Where you find one, you always find the other. And you never find one without the other, in some form or degree. They are inseparable.

R.O. McAlpine was a Wesleyan Methodist evangelist from Winston-Salem, North Carolina. He was by nature a quiet, unassuming and humble man, but when he entered the pulpit, the fire blazed. He carried a special anointing about him that was noticeable to all.

My friend, Jonathan Lewis, served as the pastor of R.O. McAlpine's home church. After the old preacher had passed on, his influence continued to permeate that congregation. Jonathan said that when he heard the men of the church pray, he could hear R.O. McAlpine in their prayers.

When I was in college, my dad was pastoring the Free Grace Wesleyan Church at Harkers Island, North Carolina. I was home for the weekend, and it happened to be during a revival meeting with "Brother McAlpine" as we called him, doing the preaching. I was glad to get to be there and experience it.

After the evening service, we had come over to the parsonage, had enjoyed some fellowship and refreshments, and were relaxing before retiring for the night. I was sitting in the den, reading the day's newspaper. Suddenly, I felt my foot being lifted and placed on a wooden box. I peered around the paper to see what in the world could be happening, and to my shock, there was this highly revered evangelist kneeling at my feet starting to polish my shoe! And as he continued, he began to weep and pray for me and my future in ministry.

I weep now as I relive that memory.

What an act of humble love that was. And how humbling it was to be receiving such a blessing. I have never forgotten it, or gotten over it. Every time I think of humility, I think of that man and that experience.

I later found out that it was one of his customs to offer such a gift of humble love to other pastors, and those who received that gift always expressed the same sense of humble gratitude that I experienced.

I also remember hearing another old evangelist in the Holiness Movement, John Sutherland Logan, express, "There is a world of difference between being humble and being humiliated." The unfortunate reality behind this statement is that, in his experience and many of ours, there were any number of spiritually prideful people who wrongly assumed it was their calling from God to keep the rest of us in our place. And they approached that calling with zeal, using humiliation as their major weapon of enforcement.

I remember one dear lady (not the one you're thinking of, it was another one) who was known for two things. First, she was the wife of a well-known holiness evangelist. Second, she had a caustic, critical spirit. Some of us wondered — shame on us — if her husband's calling to be a traveling evangelist might not have come from a desire to be away from her. If so, John Wesley would certainly commiserate with the poor fellow.

125

She used that critical spirit to force compliance to her standard of behavior and dress, intimidating others and stealing their joy. She could humiliate you in a heartbeat.

True holiness, however, is marked by a humility of spirit that finds a way to love others as they are, and continue to love them to Jesus, who alone is charged with helping them conform to his character and behavior.

We must gently help this generation learn how to serve in holiness, which is the compelling force, and serve in humility, which is the compassionate spirit.

CHAPTER TWENTY-FIVE

THE CRUCIFIED LIFE

One of the prevailing images used in the American Holiness Movement to communicate the costly realities of the sanctified life was the image of crucifixion. Death to self, they called it.

Among holiness people, the standard teaching was that in order to be wholly sanctified, a person should take it by faith, like their salvation experience, and depend on the assurance of the work being done in the heart, as taught by John Wesley. This was a cardinal teaching of Phoebe Palmer early in the American Holiness Movement – "the altar sanctifies the gift." There was a group among the Pilgrim Holiness churches and preachers that took a much more severe approach to the sanctification process. They taught that you had to take "the death route" to be sanctified. My friend, Ernest Mullins, remembers being told he had to die like an old yellow dog. This severe teaching led to a hurtful parting of ways between old friends in the 1930s, as the Pilgrim Holiness Church had to help one of their longtime leaders stop doing that. He chose to hold to his strong convictions and departed the church with several pastors and churches following him, and most of the faculty and students of one of the Pilgrim Bible colleges pulling out, as well.

While the "death route" doctrine was extreme and officially deemed counter to solid holiness teaching as embodied in *The Manual* of the Pilgrim Holiness Church, there is a call upon us all to die to ourselves and come alive in Christ.

127

All Christians, of course, are familiar with the historic events surrounding the death of Jesus and are accustomed to seeing the form of the cross. But not all are aware of the demand for their own crucifixion event. But Jesus was crystal clear, "If any of you wants to be my follower, you must give up your own way, take up your cross, and follow me." Matthew 16:24 NLT

The Apostle Paul, in a testimony of how he saw this demand applied to his own life as a follower of Jesus, said it this way:

> "I have been crucified with Christ, and it is no longer I who live, but Christ who lives in me, and the life I now live in the flesh, I live by faith in the Son of God, who loved me and gave himself for me."
>
> Galatians 2:20 NIV

I remember when this verse first gripped my heart. I was a junior in college, sitting in Dr. W.L. Surbrook's systematic theology class. Interestingly, Dr. Surbrook was the General Superintendent in the 1930s, who had to confront his friend about the errant teaching and strive to hold the church together as it threatened to splinter.

One of the students read this verse. I am sure I had heard it before, but on this day I was arrested in my tracks.

I remember two things about that experience. First, I remember being stricken by the beauty and the boldness of those words. They are so dramatic and descriptive, holding to such a high view of the promise we have in this life. And yet, they bear such a heavy message of the cost of living that life. You have to die to live that life.

That was the second impact on me. I had been a believer since childhood, had answered a call to preach, and was in college preparing to fulfill that calling. But in conviction, I knew I was not living the life Paul was talking about. I was definitely living it "my own way" and knew I was not prepared, in that moment, to live it any other way.

I wanted to be a Christian, a preacher even — but I did not want to be crucified.

Over time, the Lord in his grace and mercy, brought me to that point of surrender. And has mercifully, but insistently, brought me back to that point many times. And the life I now live in the flesh, I live by faith in the Son of God, who loves me and gave himself for me.

C.T. Studd understood this concept all too well. He was a foreign missionary, first to China, working with Hudson Taylor, and then for the greater balance of his life to the Congo. He had been raised a child of privilege in Great Britain. He was a nationally acclaimed athlete. But he came under conviction when his father got saved through the ministry of D.L. Moody. Eventually, he also became a believer and when he did, he went all in. As a result, he lived a life of extreme sacrifice in order to fulfill the calling God laid on his heart. His story is a true inspiration.

He is known for his declaration, "Some want to live within the sound of church or chapel bell; I want to run a rescue shop within a yard of hell."

His calling required him, for long periods of time, to be separated from his family — him living on the frontlines of a dangerous place in need of the gospel, while his wife and family members remained back in England raising prayer and financial support for his work. It was a lonely and costly existence.

Studd was asked one time how he could make such sacrifices. He replied, "If Jesus Christ be God and died for me, then no sacrifice can be too great for me to make for him."

That sentiment sums up the crucified life.

And it sums up the life dream of John Wesley for all those who bear the name of Christ, especially those of us who find ourselves in his theological family.

"O that God would give me the thing which I long for! That before I go hence and am no more seen, I may see a people wholly devoted to God, crucified to the world, and the world crucified to them; a people truly given up to God, in body, soul, and substance! How cheerfully should I then say, 'Now lettest thou thy servant depart in peace.'" (Sermon, *The Danger of Riches*, 1 Timothy 6:9)

Those are high expectations. So high, they may seem foreign to us and fall harshly on our ears. But in light of who Jesus is, and what he has done, is it not reasonable that we would be a people wholly devoted to God?

I expect that of myself in my marriage. Why would my relationship with my Savior be less?

CHAPTER TWENTY-SIX

THE ANOINTING

I can't tell you how many times in my life that I have been the Monday donkey.

On the Monday after the procession into Jerusalem which we call Palm Sunday, can't you imagine that young donkey parading around the barnyard, expecting deference from all the other barnyard critters, and wondering where everyone went with the palm branches and cloaks strewn along the path? After all, he was still the same donkey. What changed?

What changed is, Jesus was there yesterday, but not today.

In the American Holiness Movement, great value was placed on what they called the anointing. It was the blessing of God placed on a person or event that made that person or event indescribably more than they or it could have been in themselves or itself. When this blessing was present, it was evident to all except the most insensible. The anointing settled down on the people like the Old Testament image of the oil flowing down over Aaron's head and shoulders, running off his beard and down his clothing, pooling at his feet. That which is intangible becomes almost tangible.

I have experienced that from time to time. I remember hearing some of my heroes preach under the anointing – people like Earle Wilson, Melvin Snyder and P.O. Carpenter, I've heard J.R. Mitchell thunder, J. Wesley Adcock preach with boldness and conviction, and the

131

Scotsman John Sutherland Logan in his sweet way invite people to come to the altar and tell Jesus how much they love him. I've seen the glory fall on Methodist preachers Dennis Kinlaw, Robert Coleman and John R. Church, as well as Baptist preacher Henry Blackaby. Bob McCluskey would have you laughing one minute and crying the next. I was in the room the night John Maxwell prayed the glory down on the Wesleyan Youth leaders. I've seen the anointing rest on Jimmy Johnson, Jo Anne Lyon and Paul Rees. In our own setting on the NC East District, I have seen the Lord settle down upon Kerry Willis, Isaac Smith, Ernest Mullins and Anthony Graham. The sparks were flying the year we turned Camp Meeting over to the Young Guns. Matt LeRoy, Josh LeRoy, Matt Smith and Luke Jackson brought the fire! I also remember the week when we were blessed by the convicting urgency of Joanne Solis Walker, the deep earnestness of Anthony Smith, and the unbounded energy of Sid Wheatley. Then it was Michael Trogdon's turn.

Michael Trogdon is a Church of God pastor who was invited to preach the closing night of that District Camp Meeting. Following the leading of the Spirit, he passed up an opportunity to showcase his considerable preaching skills and humbly invited people who needed healing to come forward for prayer. The aisles filled with people patiently waiting for the laying on of hands and anointing with oil. It was one of the most powerfully anointed services I have ever witnessed.

I never got to hear our Pilgrim Holiness or Wesleyan Methodist spiritual ancestors preach, but I understand Lucius Matlack was quite a powerful preacher, and Adam Crooks' preaching stirred up the whole State of North Carolina in such a way that they ran him out of town and back to Ohio. So from there he stirred up a whole nation with his anointed writings in *The True Wesleyan*. Seth C. Rees, the Earth Quaker, and Martin Wells Knapp with his *Lightning Bolts from Pentecostal Skies*, were anointed forces to be reckoned with at the turn of the Twentieth Century. Anointing was central to the formation and growth of our Church.

And who could forget our favorite holiness orators, Wingrove Taylor and James Earl Massey. Or the stable of evangelists from the Church of Christ in Christian Union who preached in many Wesleyan Camp Meetings and local church revivals? Men like Don Humble, Don Peiffer, Morton Dorsey, Melvin Maxwell, John Conley and others.

I've known whole families who seemed to carry with them a special anointing from the Lord. There is one in particular that started with Free Will Baptist turned Methodist preacher Jack Tyson, whose six sons – Dewey, Tommy, George, Earl, Vernon and Bobby – all became Methodist preachers. Tommy was a good friend of Oral Roberts and was greatly used of God to help Roberts' ministry thrive. This unusual family anointing has continued down into the fourth generation. I cannot explain that, but it has been amazing to witness.

I have experienced the anointing of God on my own life as a leader, certainly not to the dynamic extent as the others I have mentioned, and definitely because I desperately needed it if I was going to come close to getting the job done.

On the day of my election as District Superintendent, an issue came up on the Conference floor regarding an incident at our youth camp the summer before. At that time, I had been the person overseeing the camp ministry as Assistant District Superintendent. I had acted immediately to resolve the issue in an effective and proper manner. But I totally mishandled the concerns of a family in the District, good friends of mine, and it caused considerable tension between us.

When the Victory Mountain Camp report was given, one of the family members, my friend Dan, whom I dearly love and I know loves me, rose to ask me respectfully for a public explanation regarding my handling of the incident. I calmly replied that there were three things that needed to be shared with the Conference and proceeded to share concern number one and concern number two. Then my mind went blank. Immediately, as I panicked on the inside, the voice of the Accuser spoke loudly and with derision into my heart. "Look at you. You're supposed to be the District Superintendent and you're not even smart enough to remember three simple things." I felt the humiliation. The uncomfortable silence on the Conference floor meant everyone else felt it, too.

As I cried out in my spirit to God, a calm anointing settled upon me. I relaxed, leaned back in my seat, smiled and said to my friend, "I'm sorry, Dan. For the life of me, I can't remember the third thing! As soon as I remember it, I'll share it with you." The Conference laughed with me and we moved on. I still haven't remembered the third thing, but I'll never forget that moment of anointing. There was a clear assurance in my heart that as long as I served in that office, I would have the Lord's presence and help with me.

That anointing did not make me a perfect leader, and I had my share of mishaps. But I was definitely a better District Superintendent than I would have been without the Lord's anointing.

I'm the Monday donkey, now. I retired and the anointing for that ministry retired with me. My friends wish I had retained at least a small portion of it, I'm sure, but it's gone. I have what I need for who I am now, for which I am grateful, but I fondly remember when the Lord helped me in so many special ways.

The anointing for service is a part of the sanctifying work the Holy Spirit does in our lives. And it is to be highly valued and guarded. It was Oswald Chambers, a holiness hero of another generation (excuse the dated language), who emphasized the necessity for anointing in ministry and the awe with which we should regard it.

> "There is no limit to what God can do with a man, if he touch not the glory."

(My mom and Kerry Willis' mom both say that is a quote from Oswald Chambers, but neither Kerry nor I seem to be able to find it, so I say, it certainly sounds like him and if he didn't say it, he should have, and most likely would have if he had thought of it.)

Guard the anointing on your life and pass the glory to Jesus always.

CHAPTER TWENTY-SEVEN

SEEKING THE EXPERIENCE

It was common in the churches of the American Holiness Movement for persons to be encouraged to seek "the experience" of sanctification. Especially those young in the faith. This was done regularly with evangelistic zeal. It was part of the warp and woof of the holiness culture. It was an essential piece of the foundation of the movement, in their minds. It was a major piece of the strategy to keep "the experience" alive in the life of the holiness churches.

Which was praiseworthy in terms of the purity of their motivations, and it worked by and large to bring people into a closer and deeper sanctifying relationship with the Lord. But it was backward.

I was at a conference recently where there was a presentation on our holiness heritage followed by a question and answer period. One of the persons who came to the microphone was an educator in a school that maintains an intentional "holiness" culture. He shared that in giving students counsel regarding the sanctified life, he tells them, "Do not seek 'the experience'. Seek Jesus. By seeking Jesus, you will find that in your relationship with him, he will lead you into the experience." I find those words to be words of wisdom.

Take marriage for example.

I have friends, guys mostly, who wanted to get married so they went looking for a wife. And for most of them, it worked out just fine. But for some, sadly, that approach led to a total disaster for them. They had it all backward.

The way the process is designed to work is, boy meets girl and they fall head-over-heels in love with each other which naturally leads to marriage and, hopefully, a happy and fulfilling life.

Seek the person, not the experience.

It is like the plaque we have displayed in our home: "The secret is not to find someone you can live with, but someone you can't live without."

There is a foundational element to the life of holiness that is about propositional truth, but he driving element of the life of holiness is that it is relational and dynamic. It is something to be learned, yes.

But it is mostly something to be lived.

Seek not for sanctification. Rather, seek the Sanctifier. He is faithful, and he will do it.

CHAPTER TWENTY-EIGHT

SHOUTING AND SPEAKING IN TONGUES

The holiness folk were known to shout. Whenever they were moved to ecstatic expression of their experience, whenever "the Spirit moved" in such a way they were blessed to overflowing, they would shout, and even run the aisles. Not all of them, but enough of them that it became a characteristic for which they were known. It was a common occurrence in the camp meetings in which the movement was birthed and raised, and even common among their Methodist cousins at one time. This characteristic was carried over in the DNA of the holiness churches.

If you didn't shout and run the aisles, you were not shamed for that. But the ones who did were appreciated by those who did not.

Their Pentecostal cousins did the same thing. When so moved by the Spirit, they shouted and ran the aisles. But they also spoke in tongues. Not all of them, but unlike the holiness folk, speaking in tongues was expected and seen as a sign of having been filled with the Spirit, which was a third work of grace as taught by the Pentecostals.

There was no speaking in tongues among the holiness churches. In fact, and sadly so, that was cause for breaking fellowship with someone.

To the outside observer, there would not have been a nickel's worth of difference between the ecstatic expressions of the two groups. And if you "turned the sound down" so to speak, even the most inside of the insiders could not have told you which group was which. Now granted, the Pentecostals tended to have fringe folks who found novel and strange ways to express their ecstasy. But there were holiness people with strange ways, as well. By and large, though, the experiences and expressions were virtually identical, except for the practice of glossolalia among the Pentecostals.

I have friends from Harkers Island who, as young and exuberant, Spirit-filled believers, were prone to be very expressive in their worship, and when "in the Spirit" would whoop and holler and get pretty loud. That's just who they were and how they expressed their joy in the Lord. They made a pilgrimage to a famous holiness college to attend that school's Camp Meeting. And of course, they got blessed. The authorities at the meeting called them down in public and chastised them severely, to the humiliation of my friends. The Camp Meeting leaders, not knowing who they were or where they were from, mistook them for Pentecostals and flew into them. Of course, if you've ever heard an Islander talk, with their thick tidewater brogue, you might think they were speaking in tongues when they were just speaking the King's English. Crushed in spirit, they left the camp, drove to the home of O.W. Willis, who knew them all and had held numerous meetings at the Harkers Island church, and sought solace there. It took about all the skill and wisdom Brother Willis had to put his broken-hearted friends back together.

There would be nothing resembling Pentecostal expression allowed in a holiness meeting. And they were confident they could tell the difference.

I have said it elsewhere, and I will say it again here – what is wrong with us that we cannot have fellowship with classic Pentecostal brothers and sisters who have only one point of doctrinal difference from us. Really? I understand our differences with Charismatics and "Jesus Only" Pentecostals, but the traditional Pentecostals agree with us on every point of doctrine but one.

The holiness folk shouted and ran the aisles, but they would run you out of the church if they thought they heard you say something unintelligible to them. Honestly, I believe the world would be more inclined to accept the reality of our theology if they saw us in a spirit of love and charity sitting at the same table with our Pentecostal friends.

CHAPTER TWENTY-NINE

SOCIAL HOLINESS

The term, "social holiness", would likely never pass the lips of preacher or people in the American Holiness Movement. It just was foreign to their vocabulary.

There were two basic reasons for this. First, "social holiness" would sound too much like the "social gospel" of Walter Rauschenbusch, Washington Gladden and the like. They wouldn't touch that with a ten-foot pole. That was for the Liberals, not them.

Also, it was foreign to them because of their preoccupation with "personal holiness" which was their watchword. For them, the only holiness that mattered (apart from the glorious holiness of God) was the personal kind. Similar to a "personal relationship with Christ" which was their evangelistic appeal to lost souls, personal holiness was the logical next step in a person's walk with the Lord. The second definite work of grace subsequent to regeneration was a personal experience of the sanctifying work of God in their lives. It was very personal and powerful. And very much inward focused.

John Wesley would agree with all of that. He would object vehemently to his phrase "social holiness" being defined by the social gospel philosophy to the exclusion of the relational aspects of the life of holiness — and that seems to be what has happened in the modern version of his Methodist Connection in a majority of local churches.

And he would definitely endorse the personal aspect of faith and a person growing in their faith promoted by the American Holiness Movement.

His intention in the phrase "social holiness" is missed by both groups, however.

As previously noted, the phrase appears in the preface in a Wesley published hymnal, *Hymns and Sacred Poems* (1739), where he famously says, "The gospel of Christ knows no religion but social, no holiness but social holiness."

But what he means by that is not the liberal social gospel of improving society and so issuing in the kingdom of God on earth.

He means that woven into the plan of salvation for each of us, personal as it may be, is the critical and necessary element that our personal experience of God and our personal growth in grace is meant to take place in relationship with others on the same path.

There is no such thing as a solitary Christian, in his mind. True holiness is experienced in fellowship with others on the path, as an outwardly expressed holiness.

When I was serving as a District Superintendent, I remember writing to the pastors under my charge, on Wesley's birthday:

"Today would have been John Wesley's 312th birthday.

"As you well know, along with 'assurance of salvation,' one of the major hallmarks of Wesley's contribution to the church was his recovery of Paul's emphasis on the work of sanctification in the life of the believer.

"Here is my plea to you:

"Pastors, when you preach 'holiness,' please do not make the mistake my generation and the generations ahead of me in the American Holiness Movement made. Please remember that 'holiness' is way more than 'personal sin management.' Preach the full message of the sanctifying power of the Holy Spirit – that what he does in us and through us is internal, yes, but it is also and just as much external and relational and global, or it isn't the real thing. Any message that leaves out the relational and global aspects of 'holiness' falls short of the mark.

Thank you. And happy birthday, Grandfather John."

Do I (and Grandfather John) have scriptural support for this claim? Absolutely.

When Jesus chose to sum up the entire Law and the Prophets (and the Gospel), he said it this way:

> "Hear, O Israel: the Lord our God, the Lord is one. Love the Lord your God with all your heart and with all your soul and with all your mind and with all your strength…. Love your neighbor as yourself."
>
> Mark 12:28-31 NIV

It doesn't get any simpler or clearer than that. You don't love God if you don't also love your neighbor. It's not New Testament holiness if it doesn't get out of your heart. True holiness cannot be contained. It spills out on every person with whom we come in contact. And that contact is not just accidental or occasional. It is intentional.

And this sanctifying grace is the relational glue that holds our local churches — and the kingdom of God — together.

CHAPTER THIRTY

SELFISH AMBITION AND THE WILL OF GOD

In the summer of 1965, when I was 16 years old, my dad accepted a call to pastor the Second Pilgrim Holiness Church (later Mark Street Wesleyan, now part of Daybreak) in Marion, Ohio, in the Ohio District. We had been at the Pleasureville Pilgrim Holiness Church in the Kentucky District. We were scheduled to move to the new assignment in June, after the Kentucky District Conference.

At that District Conference on the Maysville Campgrounds, Rev. Trumble announced he was retiring as District Superintendent. In those days, every DS election was for one year and on an open ballot. How nerve-wracking was that for an incumbent?

If I remember correctly, on the first or second ballot, District hero and well-known evangelist P.O. Carpenter was elected. The Conference was elated. I think the old evangelist was in shock. He asked for a short recess so he could seek the Lord's direction. After a time of private prayer in his cottage, he reentered the tabernacle and announced in his raspy voice, to the disappointment of the crowd, that he just could not feel clear about accepting the election. He was not their man.

In the spirit of Jesus, he resisted the temptation to grasp the glory, and instead held firm to the calling that would keep him in the center of God's will for his life.

The Conference continued voting and it turned into a horse race between Pastor Paul Ebright from the Elizabethtown church and Pastor E.R. Mitchell from the Covington church. There were enough outliers drawing enough votes to keep either man from gaining a majority. This went on forever until Pastor Ebright finally squeaked out a slim majority to win the election.

This then created another dilemma, this time for my dad. The Elizabethtown church was the largest church in the District, and their delegation came to him and asked him if he would allow his name to be considered for their next pastor. Of course, there would be a whole process to go through, but they were serious in their request. As far as they were concerned, he was their man.

Chairing the Conference was the sweet-spirited General Superintendent, Dr. P.W. Thomas. Dad took his dilemma to him. Dr. Thomas listened sympathetically, asked if he had given his word to Marion, and counseled, "My brother, I know this is a difficult decision, but I would trust what God has already confirmed in your heart, and I would advise you to go to Marion and build your own Elizabethtown there."

That eased Dad's conscience and so he declined the E'town invitation and kept his commitment to Marion. I'm not surprised because that is just who he was. He was the Psalm 15 "sweareth to his own hurt, and changeth not" kind of guy. I saw that over and over in his life.

And years later when he came to the end, he stayed true to his high values. As he lay dying in the Harkers Island parsonage, Kerry Willis (now a Nazarene DS) said with sadness, "Brother LeRoy, how can I pray for you? I just can't seem to find the words." And Dad said, "Kerry, don't you worry. I've already prayed the perfect prayer: 'Not my will, but thine be done.'" My heroes lived out before me the critical importance, no matter how enticing, to choose the good, pleasing and perfect will of God, and not to fall prey to the temptation of selfish ambition.

The heart and life that is being wholly sanctified knows this well. There is no place up from the center of God's will. Every other place is a step down from there.

CHAPTER THIRTY-ONE

SAVING SOULS

Standing tall along the coast of North Carolina are our treasured claims to fame, our lighthouses. Because of the treacherous shoals and shifting sands along our shores, many sailing vessels have run aground. As a warning to ships of the perilous conditions along the Atlantic coastline, lighthouses were erected to guide the ships and guard from shipwreck.

North Carolina's seven most famous lighthouses are, from north to south:

The Currituck light is at Corolla. It is distinct from the others as it is the only one left unpainted. Finished and first put into service on December 1, 1875, this stately brick-colored structure stands 162 feet tall. It is a coastal light.

The Bodie Island light guards the Oregon Inlet. This light was built in 1872 and stands 156 feet tall. It is a harbor light, and is painted in alternating black and white horizontal stripes — three white and two black with a black illuminated superstructure.

The grande dame of the North Carolina lights is the Cape Hatteras lighthouse.

Located on the farthest east tip of the Outer Banks, the Cape Hatteras lighthouse is the tallest of the seven, standing 198 and one-half feet tall. It is the tallest brick lighthouse in the United States. It was built in 1870, and is known for its spiraling black and white design with a red and sand-colored base. It is a coastal light.

On the southwestern tip of Ocracoke Island, part of the chain of barrier islands known as the Outer Banks, stands the Ocracoke Lighthouse. It is seventy-five feet tall, and as a harbor light, helps guide ships through the Ocracoke inlet into the Pamlico Sound. It was built in 1823.

Fifty miles to the southwest is the Cape Lookout Lighthouse. Identifiable by its black and white diamond pattern – white diamonds facing east and west, black diamonds facing north and south. The Cape Lookout light was built in 1859, and stands 163 feet tall. It is a coastal light.

Farther south, near Southport, is Bald Head Island, home to the Bald Head Island Lighthouse. "Old Baldy" was built in 1817 and is the oldest lighthouse still standing in the state. It is a harbor light, marking the entrance to the Cape Fear River. Octagonal in shape, it was originally painted white, but it now bears a mottled brown, green, tan and gray stucco coloring. It stands 110 feet tall.

The last of the North Carolina lights to be built is the Oak Island Lighthouse. Located adjacent to the Coast Guard Station, the Oak Island light guards Frying Pan Shoals. Unlike the other lights, constructed of brick, this light is constructed of Portland concrete. It stands 153 feet tall and is painted, from top down, one-third black, one-third white and one-third gray.

Why am I including all this detail? Because the lives of sailors in peril on the seas were so important to the United States government that they made Herculean efforts to guide them safely home.

But standing stately and shining a light into the darkness isn't enough. We do not know how many shipwrecks were avoided because of the faithful witness of the lights along the shore, but we do know there is a massive "Graveyard of the Atlantic" filled with the remains of wrecked, sunken ships.

So the lighthouses, as important as they may have been to saving sailors, were at best a passive influence in that effort. They stood along the shoreline faithfully shining their light, but they never launched out to rescue perishing sailors.

That was left to the United States Life Saving Service, the forerunner of today's United States Coast Guard.

Starting in 1878, the United States government established Life Saving Stations along the East coast, manned by trained crews to save the lives of sailors and passengers at risk. This grew out of local volunteer efforts that had sprung up out of humanitarian concerns. You can't just stand by and watch somebody drown. You have to try to save them.

Out of that compassion and courage comes a story from the Chickamicomico station near Rodanthe. Protesting the darkness and fierceness of a storm, one of the young crew members said, "Cap'n, we cain't go out in this! We'll all be kil't!" To which the crew captain responded, "Boys, the book says we gotta go out! It don't say nuthin' 'bout comin' back!"

At the Cape Lookout station, in February of 1905, nine young life savers showed the strength of their courage and depth of their commitment.

The three-masted freight vessel, the *Sarah D.J. Rawson* had departed Georgetown, South Carolina with a load of lumber bound for New York. On Thursday, February 9, four days into their journey, at about 5:30 pm, they were caught by surprise by a roaring storm just southeast of the point at Cape Lookout. The heavy winds and driving rains, accompanied by thick fog, created a "perfect storm" situation for them. They were driven into the shoals, run aground and pinned there at the mercy of the storm — which had no mercy on them. Almost immediately, one of their eight-member crew was washed overboard, never to be seen again. The others dropped the sails and tied themselves off to the ship and hung on for dear life as it began to be beaten apart by the surging surf.

The rain and heavy fog kept the young man on watch in the tower at the Life Saving station from seeing the ship nine miles away. Sometime around noon the next afternoon, Keeper Gaskill, the lead crew member at the station, walked out into the storm, and through a break in the fog, caught sight of three masts through the driving rain. By their awkward position, he knew they had a ship aground on the shoals and sounded the alarm!

The nine-man crew sprang into action, grabbing their equipment and rolling their small lifeboat through the deep sand to the shore. They launched out into the surf, rowing nine miles through rolling waves and heavy freezing rain until they reached the grounded ship. It was around 4:00 pm by this time. Darkness would be soon approaching. They repeatedly tried to reach the wrecked ship, laying over on her starboard side, but the winds, waves and floating debris kept driving them back.

They were unable to get close enough to get their heaving rope to the ship. Any attempts to get close to the ship in the darkness and fog proved futile. Not only were they hindered by the darkness and the storm, but the seas surrounding the ship were full of parts of the ship as well as most of the lumber cargo being thrown around with force in the surging tide. This was a perilous time for everyone.

They made the tactical decision to anchor the surf boat. Close enough to launch an immediate rescue if the ship completely broke apart, but far enough away to be clear of the dangerous debris. They had no choice but to trust the strength of that rope to keep them from being swept away. Now they, like the poor sailors they were trying to rescue, were hanging on for dear life.

As if it were not already an intolerable situation, a good number of the surfmen were extremely sick with the flu.

Through the night, without food or water, thrown every which way by wind and wave, dodging deadly pieces of lumber thrown at them in the pitch black night, they hung on. This went on into the next morning and into the afternoon. Finally, with the tide turning, the storm subsided enough that they could pull themselves to the ship.

149

Then the laborious task of rescuing the sailors, a few at a time, began as the surfmen got the rope thrown to the wreckage and — one by one in the heaving surf — the sailors were hauled through the waters and placed in the safety of the little rescue dory. The surfmen even gave up their own coats in the freezing temperatures to warm the rescued sailors.

Finally, at around 5:00 that evening, more than twenty-four hours after Keeper Gaskill's call to action, every sailor and every surfman was safe on shore and sheltered in the Life Saving Station.

For their heroic actions, Keeper William H. Gaskill and Surfmen Kilby Guthrie, Walter M. Yeomans, Tyre Moore, John A. Guthrie, James W. Fulcher, John E. Kirkman, Calupt T. Jarvis and Joseph L. Lewis were awarded the Gold Life Saving Medal for "heroic daring" in the rescue of the crew of the *Sarah D.J. Rawson*.

Walter M. Yeomans, a twenty-something at the time, went on to become the great-grandfather of my wife, Cynthia Guthrie LeRoy.

Today you can visit the Cape Lookout Seashore National Park, climb the Lighthouse and explore the Cape. There you will find, weathered and beaten but still standing, the old Life Saving Station sitting quietly and abandoned among the handful of other small homes and buildings preserved in the Old Village. It may stand silent today, but for those who know, it still tells quite a story.

So what does this mean for us?

Evangelistic fervor was one of the distinguishing characteristics of the people who made up the American Holiness Movement. Spurred on by a holy love for God and a loving concern for "the lost", they were compelled to shine a light in the darkness and say a good word for Jesus. The intensity of their personal witness was tempered by each person's personality temperament, but the responsibility to bear witness was a universal trait among them. Their entire approach to how they conducted themselves — how they lived, how they looked, how they talked, how they related to others, where they went, and where they wouldn't go — was all about preserving their witness, a critical step to winning souls to Jesus.

The urgency they felt was the same urgency felt by those young rescue workers in the Life Saving Service. They saw "the lost" around them as being in just as great peril as the sailors on a sinking ship. Except this was not just about mortal life. This was about eternal life (or death).

One of the aspects of our current status that I love about us is, our churches continue to be focused on evangelism. One of the aspects I mourn about us is, our people are pretty much disengaged in the effort, content to let the preachers win the lost through their pulpit ministries.

Ninety-five per cent of our salvation army seems to feel that they have done their duty if they just show up on a somewhat regular basis for their weekend roll call, but in way too many places they are pretty much absent from meaningful battlefield engagement. The truly sanctified life always leads to sacrificial service for the salvation of others. As the sign at the old Coast Guard Station at Cape Lookout reads, "Times changed, but the job — saving lives — remained the same."

The old holiness folk understood the beauty of the words of Oswald Chambers, "So long as there is a human being who does not know Jesus Christ, I am his debtor to serve him until he does."

151

CONCLUSION

What is best? That is the Wesleyan question.

Not what is convenient or what are the rest of the folks doing? Not what is acceptable or okay? Not what would the respectable or affluent do? Not what is common current practice? Not even what is good or better? What is best? That is the Wesleyan question.

We believe that there is a life that is best for us to live, that puts us in the best relationship possible with God and others, that makes us the best people we can be, and puts us in position to make the best contribution we can make for a broken world, spinning out of control. That life is a life lived in full surrender to a good and loving God who wants to love the world in the best way through us.
That, of course, is not the only option for a Christian. But we believe it is the best one.

In his sermon, "The More Excellent Way," John Wesley makes this observation about our options in choosing our path:

> From long experience and observation I am inclined to think, that whoever finds redemption in the blood of Jesus, whoever is justified, has then the choice of walking in the higher or the lower path. I believe the Holy Spirit at that time sets before him "the more excellent way," and incites him to walk therein, to choose the narrowest path in the narrow way, to aspire after the heights and depths of holiness, — after the entire image of

God. But if he does not accept this offer, he
insensibly declines into the lower order of Christians.
He still goes on in what may be called a good way,
serving God in his degree, and finds mercy in the
close of life, through the blood of the covenant.

We believe the Holy Spirit walks with us on the path, and
draws us to the higher, more excellent way. We also believe
that, if we choose the lower path, he still walks with us on that
path and still draws our hearts to the higher, better way. The
critical question is, which path will we choose? And which
path will we encourage our family and friends to take? If the
best path leads them to their best life, don't we want to join the
Holy Spirit in his work to help them find that path? And if that
means communicating this wonderful option to them in terms
they understand and will embrace, shouldn't we, with the help
of the Holy Spirit, find a way to do that?

That is the point of this book. Following the Spirit, find the
path and find a way to bring others along with us on that path.
That is why God chose to raise up The Wesleyan Church. We
have enough religion. We have enough Evangelical churches.
We need a grace-filled holiness Church with a compelling love
for God and others, that will help people understand, there is an
answer to their question:

Is this all there is?
No. There is more. Much more.
And it is for real. It is for us. It is for now.

Made in the USA
Middletown, DE
12 April 2024

52847625R00094